TWENTIETH CENTURY VIEWS

The aim of this series is to present the best in contemporary critical opinion on major authors, providing a twentieth century perspective on their changing status in an era of profound revaluation.

Maynard Mack, *Series Editor*
Yale University

SWIFT

S W I F T

A COLLECTION OF CRITICAL ESSAYS

Edited by

Ernest Tuveson

A SPECTRUM BOOK

Prentice-Hall, Inc., *Englewood Cliffs, N. J.*

Current printing (last digit):

12   11

© 1964 BY PRENTICE-HALL, INC.

ENGLEWOOD CLIFFS, N. J.

LIBRARY OF CONGRESS CATALOG CARD NO.: 64-12238

Printed in the United States of America

C

P87950
C87951

Table of Contents

SWIFT

Introduction

by Ernest Tuveson

A collection of essays and chapters from books representing
twentieth century views of Jonathan Swift is especially appropriate,
for it could be said that he belongs to our time more than to any
other, even his own. Indeed, some aspects of his work—his political
and ecclesiastical propaganda, for example, or his satire of the
"absurdity of the human condition"—are more comprehensible to
us than they were to his own contemporaries. Even before his
death a curiously distorted and distorting opinion of his life and
works had emerged—partly encouraged, it must be confessed, by
actions on his part that helped to create a Swift legend, even as
Shaw did much to set up a misleading Shaw legend. To appreciate what has happened in the past few decades, we must start
with the traditional view that prevailed at the beginning of the
twentieth century.

Sir Walter Scott, who edited Swift's works, thought Swift was
irritability and savage indignation all compact, combined with an
extraordinary but perverse genius: we are "compelled to admire
the force of his talents, even while thus unworthily employed, in
exposing the worst parts of our nature with the art of an anatomist
dissecting a mangled and half-putrid carcase"; Swift perpetrated in
Gulliver's Travels a "libel on human nature." Thackeray, probably the most influential of nineteenth century writers on Swift,
found the "moral" of the great satire "horrible, shameful, unmanly, blasphemous; and giant and great as this Dean is, I say
we should hoot him." Those who have been so fortunate as not
to have read the fourth voyage, he advises "Don't"—don't read
this "monster gibbering shrieks and gnashing imprecations against
mankind,—tearing down all shreds of modesty, past all sense of
manliness and shame; filthy in word, filthy in thought, furious,

,

raging, obscene." The almost hysterical repetition of "unmanly" seems somehow revealing. Of the comic, which Fielding (in some ways so like Thackeray) found in Swift, we hear nothing. Almost everyone in the nineteenth century granted this perverted genius a lurid creative power, impelled though he was by demons of disappointed ambition and madness to rail against—what? Not, in reality, merely "mankind"; we soon realize that the essential difficulty is that Swift rejected the idols of the century—the faith in great movements in history, especially automatic progress, the optimism about the perfectibility of man, and the preoccupation with those "transcendentals" of which, Gulliver says, he never could get the Brobdingnagians to form any conception. There were overtones, too, of something like the Byronic hero as artist, a sublime but mysteriously evil, self-destroying figure taking out his obscure resentments on mankind. One is tempted to speculate that much of this feeling had its deepest origins in a sense of insecurity about those idols of the time. The nineteenth century had its tight orthodoxy, and like other orthodoxies, it found that its critics' heresies were due, not to original observation and frank statement, but to a morbid and possibly diabolical taint that prevented their authors from perceiving reality truly. In part, also, the revulsion from Swift was due to the singular fact that the earlier eighteenth century was in effect almost lost to view, a fact evidenced by the confused idea that Wordsworth in 1800 had of the poetry of only a few decades earlier. The period was popularly viewed as a kind of Augean stable of nastiness and coarseness, which the romantic revolution had to cleanse, and Swift was its keeper. Thus if the critical opinion of Swift was to change, there would have to be change on two fronts: there would have to be constructed a new "image" of the author himself and of his works, and there would have to be a reconstruction of his age as it really was, in its politics, ideas, and literature. The twentieth century, especially since the First World War, has in considerable measure accomplished both these feats, although it would be an exaggeration to say that all the mists have now been dissipated; but at least we are in all probability closer to Swift's ultimate meanings than was any generation before.

Significantly, the turn began to be evident after the First World War. This tremendous catastrophe and crime shattered the confidence about man's nature and future that had been the foundation of the orthodoxy to which I have referred. Both the "libel on human nature" and the mystery of its author's personality had a fascination for the Twenties; the unbalanced rebel was a hero of the decade, and Swift was recast in this image. One of the most representative figures of that decade, John Middleton Murry, in a biography and in a later essay (both cited in the Selected Bibliography, at the end of this volume), reflects the transitional attitude.

The formal thesis of Murry's essay, for example, is in line with the old interpretation, but with an ambivalence of attitude that would have puzzled Thackeray and Gosse. Swift, Murry writes, although exercising iron control over his work, was nevertheless motivated by a "destructive daimon", which produced finally a "physical nausea of mankind." Disappointed ambition is still seen as a cause for this compulsive negativism, despite the fact that Swift himself said he was a misanthrope, but not in the manner of Timon of Athens. But we find a new note, one that would have been impossible to find before: Swift's misanthropy and ultimate madness are explained psychoanalytically in terms of an intense emotional frustration sexual in origin. Yet Murry recognizes, also, that Swift was a conscious artist, intimately involved in and criticizing the manners and politics of his time; a great master of the comic, neither so gloomy nor so savage as has been thought; and a sincere believer in his religion, to whom the idea of original sin was compulsive.

Mr. Leavis, in his acute analysis of his irony, also finds Swift's incredibly brilliant and controlled technique used to project an essential negativism. "A great writer—yes; that account still imposes itself as fitting, though his greatness is no matter of moral grandeur or human centrality; our sense of it is merely a sense of great force. And this force, as we feel it, is conditioned by frustration and constriction; the channels of life have been blocked and perverted." Swift's religious conviction, of which there can be no doubt, is itself the product of his "insane egotism" and "the savagery with which he fought to maintain this cover over the void, this decent surface." Significantly (for reasons that will appear later) Mr. Leavis's critique is largely devoted to *A Tale of a Tub*. Frustration, constriction, compulsive egotism and nihilism, manifesting themselves in passionate outpourings of destructive power—and the serious artist, working with great skill to achieve precise rhetorical effects: are the two figures compatible? "He certainly does not impress us as a mind in possession of its experience," says Mr. Leavis, and yet "Swift is a great English writer." Is this strange contradiction the key to Swift? Has he something serious and important to say to our time, or is he merely a genius of destruction, who "does it to annoy"? To answer this question is perhaps the most urgent problem of Swiftian criticism at the present moment.

Sigmund Freud bestrides the twentieth century. Psychoanalysis has had a pervasive influence, not least on the interpretation of literature. Behind most psychoanalytical criticism is an assumption that not the work of an author but his unconscious mind, revealed in that work, is the real object of interest. It was inevitable that Swift should be a magnet for this kind of study. Norman O. Brown, in the second essay of this selection, gives a good brief account of the many attempts to psychoanalyze Swift, together with a trenchant critique of their faults. But he goes on to show that the discoveries of Freud and his followers can, if properly used, be of real value in studying Swift. The point is not that "Swift was mad and that his works should be read only as documents in a case history"; for "only Swift could do justice to the irony of psychoanalysts, whose capacity for finding the anus in the most unlikely places is notorious, condemning Swift for obsessive preoccupation with anality." Brown's valuable contribution is to point out that we should not try to "explain away Swift's literary achievements as mere epiphenomena on his individual neurosis," but rather "seek to appreciate his insight into the universal neurosis of mankind." There is no getting around the problem of the "scatology" of Swift, and, even when we remember that "coarse" allusions were commonplace in his time, we still have the problem of its pervasiveness and extraordinary vehemence in his work, especially in some of the poems. Mr. Brown's explanation no doubt is neither complete nor entirely correct, but it is a start. Unfortunately, the intellectual world of the twentieth century is rigidly divided. Literary critics and scholars know little about psychoanalysis, and psychoanalysts know little of literature. Cooperation, instead of the mutual hostility that has hitherto prevailed, might produce interesting results.

The first unspectacular but essential step to the recovery of Swift as a major and universally meaningful author was the construction of a truthful biography. About hardly any other writer of stature, perhaps, have so many lurid myths accumulated. The result of the work of such careful scholars as Ricardo Quintana, Louis Landa, Irvin Ehrenpreis, and others has been in a sense negative, but not for that reason the less useful. Their findings have replaced the erupting volcano with a passionate but real man, and, by establishing as far as possible what the real facts are, they have shown that Swift's works are not merely a kind of auto-biography. For example, the relationship of Swift with "Stella," which looms for Murry as a central event in explaining the satires, seems far less abnormal than it had been fancied; the secret marriage few scholars now would credit. Again, modern medicine has come to the aid of the biographer in explaining the awful mystery of the "madness." Swift suffered, it now seems likely, from Meunière's syndrome, a distressing but not mentally unbalancing disorder, and, in the last years of his life, from arteriosclerosis. That he was irascible and that he probably had some neuroses of his own, like most of the rest of us, is not improbable, but the more we know of his actions the more we appreciate the logic of his purposes and the clarity and sureness of his execution of them. Swift now emerges as a rhetorician in the classical and Renaissance tradition, who "invented" and ordered his material in a sure and workmanlike way to achieve rationally determined effects.

A surprising result of biographical investigation is the fact that this passionate man consistently desired and worked for practical, "middle of the road" solutions to problems. He prided himself on being a moderate Tory; in the fable of Martin and Jack, in *A Tale of a Tub,* he advocated the *via media* of the Church of England; *A Modest Proposal,* that masterpiece of "savage" irony, ends with a series of carefully worked proposals for the Irish to help themselves economically; he was firmly on the side of authority and established institutions, and distrusted radical proposals for sweeping reform, however enticing; and *Gulliver's Travels,* despite common impressions to the contrary, presents in every voyage a balanced picture of human nature and the presence of goodness and good sense, as well as folly and vice in each country visited. He believed, one might say, in the hard kind of compromise—not in avoiding difficult decisions, or taking the "easy way out," but in using judgment and restraint in the face of full knowledge of all the facts about people and events. Along with this attitude went an emphasis on the *practical* improvement of the human lot. Some of his bitterest satire was directed at theorists and fanatics who would place an abstract principle above commonplace needs.

Study of the literary and intellectual background of Swift has revealed more and more how varied it is. Swift had an omnivorous mind, that took into itself every kind of expression, from the classics to the Transactions of the Royal Society. As he used details from this reading, ordinary details took on a profound symbolic significance. Marjorie Nicolson and Nora Mohler have shown that the Voyage to Laputa, seemingly a pure fantasy if ever there was one, was constructed out of an intensive study of the new philosophy, and that none of the "projects" is wholly his own invention. And yet behind this marvelous Book of the Nuts is a deep and ominous warning. The Laputians, apparently so completely absorbed in pure abstraction, use their "know-how" to make a colony of Lagado; Swift saw, as hardly anyone else did in his time, the dark potentialities of the new science.

Hundreds of articles have recaptured, bit by bit, the significance of the topical allusions whose meaning had lapsed through the years. Much of this study has seemed, even to hardened Swiftians, curious rather than illuminating. But in fact this literary detective work is essential. A satirist necessarily has to express his permanent meanings through references to transient events and people. If we are to get through to the inner meaning of Swift, therefore, we must react to his topical satire, as far as possible, as would readers who bought the first editions. One notable example may be mentioned, for it is one of the most important pieces of scholarly research on Swift. The first voyage seemed for a long time to be little more than a fine story; even Johnson thought that once you had the little people and the big people, everything else followed in train. That it was a *roman à clef* became forgotten. In 1920, however, Sir Charles Firth identified the figures and episodes in Lilliput as allegories of politicians and political events in the England of Walpole's time. The wonderful skill of Swift in constructing his partisan attack became apparent, but there seemed to be little further significance. More recently, however, the research of Sir Lewis Namier has put the Book into a different light. Swift not only satirized the corruptions of Walpole, but also characterized the moral climate of a nation, a recurring aspect of man the political animal. The moral state of any nation dominated by petty struggles for power and money, in which important and unimportant become reversed, and principles steadily disintegrate— this is the underlying theme of the voyage.

Study of the intellectual history of the period has revealed that, far from being the self-satisfied "Age of the Augustans," it was a time of great revolutionary changes in thought. Old ideas of man and his nature were being replaced by conceptions of the essential goodness and rationality of the human being, symbolized by the "Noble Savage." The idea that man primitively is good, spoiled by the corruptions of civilization, is clearly contrary to Swift's observation of mankind. It is inconceivable that he was unaware of the writings of such philosophers as the third Earl of Shaftesbury, who propounded the theory that man has an innate "moral sense"; and he certainly was aware of the optimistic, mechanistic philosophy of his old friend and patron, Lord Bolingbroke. It is hard to believe that, in the picture of the Yahoo, we do not have an image of reality that contradicts the optimistic estimate of the "natural man" advanced by those who would replace the conception of "original sin"—both classical and Christian in its origins —with the ideas that were to lead to Rousseau.

How far the key to Swift had been lost may be seen in the universal assumption that everything in Swift's work somehow represents his own, direct opinion. As early as 1926, John B. Moore noted "that Gulliver is not Swift himself in either intellect or disposition." Gulliver, he thought, is a "pilgrim to Misanthropolis," who is not Everyman, but an individual dramatic character. Joseph Horrell, in the original form of his essay published in 1943, built his analysis of *Gulliver's Travels* around the progressive experiences of Gulliver, also considered as a persona.

But the crucial contribution was Ricardo Quintana's "Situational Satire in Swift." "Swift's method," Quintana pointed out, "is uniformly by way of dramatic satire. He creates a fully realized character and a fully realized world for him to move in." The situation *is* the satire. "Once the situation has been suggested, once its tone, its flavor have been given, it promptly takes command of itself and proceeds to grow and organize by virtue of its own inherent principles." Realizing this fact, we see that, for example, the king of Brobdingnag's condemnation of men as that "most pernicious race of little odious vermin" is not the saying of Swift, but an element in a conversation that presents one view of mankind: but not *the* view. And so with all of Swift—nowhere are we told what the point is, but always we observe reality through the eyes of a beholder with his own personality and his own biases. This is not to say, however, that the method is novelistic. There has unfortunately been a fashion for analyzing the personae of Swift in terms that bring him closer to James than to Juvenal. Thus the writer of *A Tale of a Tub* has been seen as an *ingénu,* a naïve figure who is unaware of the implications of what he says, as when he praises the moderns. But if we believe this, we lose Swift the satirist. The mordant wit who tells the *Tale* (certainly closest of all the personae to Swift himself) is a virtuoso of wit, speaking with first one voice, then another, sometimes mocking himself as a human being or a modern or a wit, ironically assuming one role after another in a brilliant series of parodies and proposals for improving mankind. Much of the point, and certainly most of the artistic mastery, disappear unless we are aware always of what he is doing and aware, too, that he knows we know.

If the possibilities of situational analysis have not been properly exploited yet, another literary approach has also not received its due: the tracing of thematic unities within individual works and within Swift's whole work. The significance of similarities between situations has not been fully recognized. I have mentioned Jack's madness, in *A Tale of a Tub,* when he rips out all the finery on his cloak, thus ruining it; this situation, in its dramatic essence, reappears when Gulliver, returned from the land of the Houyhnhnms, insists on ripping out all the Yahoo in mankind.

Application of these methods might also expose a fallacy from which much Swift criticism has suffered: what might be called "unitary" interpretation—the insistence that there is only one point in each work. Thus the first and second voyages are arranged in a symmetrical pattern. Lilliput is obviously the land of pettiness, duplicity, and frivolous corruption, contrasted with Brobdingnag, the country of magnanimity and large vision. But in fact in Lilliput there is an act of nobility, when "a considerable person at court" warns Gulliver of his impending fall, and in Brobdingnag we find examples of that purposeless, thoughtless, sadistic cruelty which is one of the most depressing characteristics of human nature. This "unitary" attitude lies behind a crucial controversy of the past few years—about the "correct" interpretation of the critical fourth voyage. There has been a search for the one explanation that would unlock its meaning, and, by extension, that of Swift's whole vision of man. The old question as to whether Swift was essentially a negator, a complete pessimist, has been raised again. Thus, the argument runs, if the Yahoos represent human nature as evil, this must be the whole point, and if we admit there is also evidence of potentialities for goodness, Swift becomes a "compromiser," and the Book is merely inconsistent. Swift could not have been thinking, in writing this voyage, of the new ideas about human nature and their conflict with the older Christian tradition of original sin, because the work seems to be naturalistic, and he nowhere mentions deism or Christianity. If the Houyhnhnms are presented as ideal in certain respects, they must be wholly and completely ideal in contrast with Yahoos, and we are not justified in finding something both distasteful and comic about their imperturbable, oblivious rationality. If the Yahoos are irrational, the point must similarly be that man is irrational; it is a matter of either/or.

The reasoning behind these notions is understandable. Ordinary satire usually makes clear and unmistakable points, a firm standard, either stated or clearly implied, being set up against the lamentable state of affairs. But Swift is like Shakespeare in that he transcends the ordinary writer. Just as there is no single "meaning" of *Lear*, but many interrelated and probably paradoxical ones, so there is no single "meaning" of *Gulliver*. Swift presents a great comprehensive image of human beings in society, and of the inner nature of man, and, it is reasonable to suppose, expects us to apply them in many ways. Both Shakespeare and Swift convey a sense of the complexity and ultimately unstatable (in abstract terms) mystery of man. Gulliver's "concrete experience," Horrell says, gives "the feel or sense of life." The function of literature, whatever its genre, at its highest is to give this "sense or feel" of experience as a whole, for which we are aware of a need since we know in our hearts that no philosophy, however profound, ever plucks out the heart of our mystery. This is not to say that a vision of life need be foggy or ineffable; on the contrary, we may make many illuminating comments, as long as we are clear about not assuming in our pride that we have grasped the whole in one formula. So, in regard to *Gulliver*, we must remember that, if we look at human experience steadily and whole, it is neither all good nor all bad. To make Swift a consistent pessimist is in effect to reduce his stature as a creative artist; the great achievement is to present both viewpoints as part of a greater whole.

Irvin Ehrenpreis has shown that a central issue in Swift's satire is that of definitions. It certainly is central in the fourth voyage. The agonizing question for Gulliver is, What is it to be human? If his solution is wrong—that to be human is to be a Yahoo—we must not expect Swift to furnish us with a neat substitute. For, as Ehrenpreis says, "The problem of a moralist like Swift is less to re-define man in terms of new ideals than to knock down the fences around an accepted definition, compelling men both to measure themselves by this and to re-examine it." How does Swift go about doing this?

To begin with, we ought to rid ourselves of the lingering notion that Swift's "savage onslaught on human nature" is per se unique. Bitter attacks on general human behavior are so common that several thick volumes could be filled with them. It has been shown, for example, that the physical features of the Houyhnhnms are literal embodiments of metaphors of human sinfulness commonly employed in sermons. Indeed it might well be expected that, at the end of a universal satire of human faults, there should be the old and curiously comfortable conclusion that "only man is vile." Such attacks have had a popularity of a kind. We may feel our superiority to the common herd in being able to acknowledge such a bitter truth. The psychiatrist might speculate that in agreeing with the melancholy conclusion that man is the worst of the animals we relieve our resentments against the way we have been treated, and even have a sense of doing penance for our own feelings of guilt.

The fourth voyage, however, is something different from the regulation outpouring which says that "man is vile." Why has it, for so many years, got deeper under the skin of readers than almost any other work? The reason may be found in part comparing it with a book that probably was a source for the Houyhnhnms— Gelli's *Circe,* more or less translated by Tom Brown and published in 1702. Ulysses, conversing with a horse who was formerly a man, finds that the ex-man does not want to be remetamorphosed. His reason is that horses fulfill their nature better than man does his; they have more fortitude and temperance because they are less handicapped by the lower parts of their nature. Yet, as Ulysses points out, they lack the supreme faculty of "right reason," and are in consequence inferior in status to man.

That is to say, the failure of man is a willful failure; by virtue of his form, the kind of mind and soul he has, and so forth, he is intrinsically superior to all animals, and each human being is *in esse* rational and related to the angels. The lament is that he fails to exercise his noble faculties; but the qualities are there, and his place on the chain of being—for Gelli—is secure. But Swift lived at a time when the great modern questioning of man's place in nature was beginning. Ehrenpreis and Rosalie Colie have shown how penetratingly Locke had analyzed the old clichés, on which Western moral philosophy had been built, about the word "human." Added to this questioning were the first uneasy stirrings of the biological revolution, with its breaking down of the barrier that had always been supposed to exist between man and beast. In the background of *Gulliver* were descriptions of the orangutan, that interesting animal which was to become a kind of mascot of the eighteenth century philosophers of man. Was there here a man-beast, an anomaly certain to raise grave questions about the dignity in which the human being had been wrapped? Eighteenth century theories of evolution were to make much of the possibility that men had in some manner evolved out of the higher primates; Swift hints at a reverse process in the origin of the Yahoos. What Gulliver seems to discover is not that men often weakly yield to the importunities of their lower natures and thus forfeit their great inheritance, but that the lower nature is the very essence, the form of the human being. It could be said that therefore he went behind Renaissance rationalism to the pristine doctrine of original sin—a taint in human nature which is truly "original" and therefore the "natural" endowment of each man. In terms of modern biology, the Yahoo may be a dominant characteristic, and the good and decent a recessive one. A peculiarity of the human animal, however, is that "social evolution" is possible; the recessive character can by the influence of such civilizing elements as religion and government, traditional wisdom, family, and so on, be strengthened to the point where it governs actual conduct; but, left to himself, man will revert to the behavior of his dominant element, as do all too many European Yahoos. Swift himself put it in the jargon of his time when he wrote Pope that the definition of man as *"animal rationale"* is false, and that "it should be only *rationis capax*."

Suppose we look at the question in terms of the twentieth century. We all have said that the crimes of the Nazis were "inhuman." By our almost instinctive use of this word, we betray the fact that we erect a barrier between such monsters and ourselves; they are aberrations, evil mutations, and really outside the species. In vain have theologians tried to bring home the fact that what happened in Germany manifests a mass guilt from which no Western people is free. On the other hand, we speak of compassionate behavior as "humane." We evaluate actions according to these definitions of ourselves, not vice versa. A Houyhnhnm, for instance, might find a most puzzling ambiguity about the meaning of "humane" in this item, from the June 27, 1963, issue of *The New York Times:*

> Death can be dealt to a bull elephant in a number of ways, some of which are wretched. But the sportsman with a sense of responsibility exerts every effort to make his kill of the largest land mammal instantaneous and humane. Such a magnificent animal deserves a good death.

Suppose we were required, like Gulliver, to give a being outside our civilization a brief account of the great historical events of our century. What a heap of treacheries, colossal wars, mass tortures, and murders we should have to relate! And we should have to confess that these things were done, not by a few deranged tyrants, but in response to national hysteria and hatred. The outsider might well remark that the concentration camp is a good example of man's *humanity* to man. A powerful satire could be created around this point. We should have arrived at Gulliver's conclusion about the true nature of man; once our defense, our faith in the definition of "human," had been stripped away, we could hardly fail to see the Yahoo everywhere, even in our most respected friends.

Such a conclusion, however natural and however justifiable, is not the whole truth. If our time has exceeded all others in vicious horrors, there is the curious fact also that in every part of daily life we have seen the growth of a much keener sensitivity to suffering and injustice than ever existed before. The crooked cross of the swastika and the Red Cross are both emblems of our period. We then must ask: which is human—Hitler or Gandhi? The only truly realistic answer is—both. Here we encounter a great difficulty; the human mind is so constructed that it always requires logical solutions. To say that man is simultaneously evil and good in his nature evokes a kind of frustration, a psychological state perhaps not unlike claustrophobia. Hence one reason for the popularity of either unrelieved pessimism or unrelieved optimism.

If Gulliver, after leaving Houyhnhnmland, had encountered scoundrels like the pirates who put him adrift, the book would have the consistency that many readers have insisted on attributing to it. But, as John Ross pointed out in his revolutionary article, "The Final Comedy of Lemuel Gulliver," the book ends very differently. Gulliver encounters true kindness in the person of Don Pedro, and the family scene at the end is suitable for the most conventional Victorian novel—all but Gulliver, cowering apart, obsessed with Yahoos. And in the Letter to Sympson (curiously neglected by most students of Swift) we see him as a humor character—a self-deluded fanatical reformer; the tone of his letter, querulous, crotchety, disorganized, is noticeably different from the sober and clear style of the narration itself. He has become a neurotic, who has lost his usefulness in his calling to society.

Thus Swift, after seeming to set up a formula and prepare us, like Houyhnhnms (with whom, following Gulliver, we naturally associate ourselves), to canter down the road after him to a readily foreseeable solution, suddenly changes course, and leaves us bewildered about where he is going. Why?

It has been said that Swift's meaning is that man is part Houyhnhnm and part Yahoo, the two so to speak alternating. Perhaps that is too mild. The point perhaps is that the deepest, the primeval human being in us is symbolized by the Yahoo. When man—any man—behaves simply and nakedly as a human, he is likely to be a Yahoo. Those who defined man as "rational" believed that he behaves reasonably (which means far more than merely logically) unless deflected—the Renaissance moralists would say, by weakly yielding to his passions; while the followers of Shaftesbury would say that man's innate sense of the good and beautiful is often warped by false education and the influence of institutions. Swift's point seems to be that man at heart is the Yahoo, but that he can be deflected or shaped into something fairly good and decent. The Europeans do have the scent of the Yahoo, and that paragon of human nature, the king of Brobdingnag, understands perfectly the real corruption of England, whereas the Houyhnhnm master, who is outside human nature, cannot conceive it.

I would suggest that the experience of Gulliver is monitory. Swift had learned much in the decades that elapsed between *A Tale of a*

Tub and *Gulliver*. The Digressions in the former, that great exposé of the "absurdity of the human condition," end on a note of nihilism: " . . . to write upon *Nothing;* when the subject is utterly exhausted, to let the pen still move on; by some called the ghost of wit, delighting to walk after the death of its body." But the ending of *Gulliver* is, I think, if we really appreciate it, something more useful. What happens to Gulliver is a warning, and a psychological preparation for us, the readers. We, too, if we are to encounter human nature in its spiritual nakedness, must see clearly all its potentialities for evil, without the protections of our proud estimate of what it is to be "human." But, having encountered it, we must be, as Thackeray would say, "manly" enough not to yield to the despair that crushes Gulliver; our job is to strengthen the potentialities for good which, though weak and often defeated, do in fact exist. Having vicariously followed Gulliver through his pilgrimage, we vicariously share his despair, but we also observe his collapse, and take warning therefrom. The result is what might be called a "satiric catharsis"; to put it another way, *Gulliver* is an initiation into a wise and productive misanthropy. Quintana has stated the matter very well: "The burden of civilization can be borne solely by such as have learned that human dignity is achieved not through hope but through willful disillusion, acceptance, resolution." Through these stages we must pass in our own dark time if we are to escape the despair or cynicism that sometimes seem inevitable. Swift holds up before us a glass in an eighteenth century frame; but if we will, we can see in it our twentieth century faces.

The Irony of Swift

by F. R. Leavis

Swift is a great English writer. For opening with this truism I have a reason: I wish to discuss Swift's writings—to examine what they are; and they are (as the extant commentary bears witness) of such a kind that it is peculiarly difficult to discuss them without shifting the focus of discussion to the kind of man that Swift was. What is most interesting in them does not so clearly belong to the realm of things made and detached that literary criticism, which has certainly not the less its duties toward Swift, can easily avoid turning—unawares, and that is, degenerating—into something else. In the attempt to say what makes these writings so remarkable, reference to the man who wrote is indeed necessary; but there are distinctions. For instance, one may (it appears), having offered to discuss the nature and import of Swift's satire, find oneself countering imputations of misanthropy with the argument that Swift earned the love of Pope, Arbuthnot, Gay, several other men and two women: this should not be found necessary by the literary critic. But the irrelevancies of Thackeray and of his castigator, the late Charles Whibley—irrelevancies not merely from the point of view of literary criticism—are too gross to need placarding; more insidious deviations are possible.

The reason for the opening truism is also the reason for the choice of title. To direct the attention upon Swift's irony gives, I think, the best chance of dealing adequately, without deviation or confusion, with what is essential in his work. But it involves also (to anticipate an objection) a slight to the classical status of *Gulliver's Travels,* a book which, though it may represent Swift's most impressive achievement in the way of complete creation—the thing achieved and detached—does not give the best opportunities for examining his irony. And *Gulliver's Travels,* one readily agrees, hasn't its classical status for nothing. But neither is it for nothing that, suitably abbreviated, it has become a classic for children. What for the adult reader constitutes its peculiar force—what puts it in so different a class from *Robinson Crusoe*—resides for the most part in the fourth book (to a less extent in the third). The adult may re-read the first two parts, as he may *Robinson Crusoe,* with great interest, but his interest, apart from being more critically conscious, will not be of a different order from the child's. He will, of course, be aware of an ingenuity of political satire in *Lilliput,* but the political satire is, unless for historians, not very much alive today. And even the more general satire characteristic of the second book will not strike him as very subtle. His main satisfaction, a great deal enhanced, no doubt, by the ironic seasoning, will be that which Swift, the student of the *Mariner's Magazine* and of travelers' relations, aimed to supply in the bare precision and the matter-of-fact realness of his narrative.

But what in Swift is most important, the disturbing characteristic of his genius, is a peculiar emotional intensity; that which, in *Gulliver,* confronts us in the Struldbrugs and the Yahoos. It is what we find ourselves contemplating when elsewhere we examine his irony. To lay the stress upon an emotional intensity should be matter of commonplace: actually, in routine usage, the accepted word for Swift is "intellectual." We are told, for instance, that his is preeminently "intellectual satire" (though we are not told what satire is). For this formula the best reason some commentators can allege is the elaboration of analogies—their "exact and elaborate propriety" [1]—in *Gulliver.* But a muddled perception can hardly be expected to give a clear account of itself; the stress on Swift's "intellect" (Mr. Herbert Read alludes to his "mighty intelligence")[2] registers, it would appear, a confused sense, not only of the mental exercise involved in his irony, but of the habitually critical attitude he maintains toward the world, and of the negative emotions he specializes in.

From "critical" to "negative" in this last sentence is, it will be observed, a shift of stress. There are writings of Swift where

[1] Churton Collins.
[2] *English Prose Style.*

"critical" is the more obvious word (and where "intellectual" may seem correspondingly apt)—notably, the pamphlets or pamphleteering essays in which the irony is instrumental, directed and limited to a given end. The *Argument Against Abolishing Christianity* and the *Modest Proposal,* for instance, are discussible in the terms in which satire is commonly discussed: as the criticism of vice, folly, or other aberration, by some kind of reference to positive standards. But even here, even in the *Argument,* where Swift's ironic intensity undeniably directs itself to the defense of something that he is intensely concerned to defend, the effect is essentially negative. The positive itself appears only negatively—a kind of skeletal presence, rigid enough, but without life or body; a necessary pre-condition, as it were, of directed negation. The intensity is purely destructive.

The point may be enforced by the obvious contrast with Gibbon —except that between Swift's irony and Gibbon's the contrast is so complete that any one point is difficult to isolate. Gibbon's irony, in the fifteenth chapter, may be aimed against, instead of for, Christianity, but contrasted with Swift's it is an assertion of faith. The decorously insistent pattern of Gibbonian prose insinuates a solidarity with the reader (the implied solidarity in Swift is itself ironical —a means to betrayal), establishes an understanding, and habituates to certain assumptions. The reader, it is implied, is an eighteenth century gentleman ("rational," "candid," "polite," elegant," "humane"); eighteen hundred years ago he would have been a pagan gentleman, living by these same standards (those of absolute civilization); by these standards (present everywhere in the stylized prose and adroitly emphasized at keypoints in such phrases as "the polite Augustus," "the elegant mythology of the Greeks") the Jews and early Christians are seen to have been ignorant fanatics, uncouth and probably dirty. Gibbon as a historian of Christianity had, we know, limitations; but the positive standards by reference to which his irony works represent something impressively realized in eighteenth century civilization; impressively "there" too in the grandiose, assured, and ordered elegance of his history. (When, on the other hand, Lytton Strachey, with a Gibbonian period or phrase or word, a "remarkable," "oddly," or "curious," assures us that he feels an amused superiority to these Victorian puppets, he succeeds only in conveying his personal conviction that he feels amused and superior.)

Gibbon's irony, then, habituates and reassures, ministering to a kind of judicial certitude or complacency. Swift's is essentially a matter of surprise and negation; its function is to defeat habit, to intimidate, and to demoralize. What he assumes in the *Argument* is not so much a common acceptance of Christianity as that the reader will be ashamed to have to recognize how fundamentally un-christian his actual assumptions, motives, and attitudes are. And in general the implication is that it would shame people if they were made to recognize themselves unequivocally. If one had to justify this irony according to the conventional notion of satire, then its satiric efficacy would be to make comfortable non-recognition, the unconsciousness of habit, impossible.

A method of surprise does not admit of description in an easy formula. Surprise is a perpetually varied accompaniment of the grave, dispassionate, matter-of-fact tone in which Swift delivers his intensities. The dissociation of emotional intensity from its usual accompaniments inhibits the automatic defense-reaction:

> He is a Presbyterian in politics, and an atheist in religion; but he chooses at present to whore with a Papist.

> What bailiff would venture to arrest Mr. Steele, now he has the honour to be your representative? and what bailiff ever scrupled it before?

—Or inhibits, let us say, the normal response; since "defence" suggests that it is the "victim" whose surprise we should be contemplating, whereas it is our own, whether Swift's butt is Wharton or the atheist or mankind in general. "But satire, being leveled at all, is never resented for an offence by any, since every individual makes bold to understand it of others, and very wisely removes his particular part of the burden upon the shoulders of the World, which are broad enough and able to bear it." [3] There is, of course, no contradiction here; a complete statement would be complex. But, actually, the discussion of satire in terms of offense and castigation, victim and castigator, is unprofitable, though the idea of these has to be taken into account. What we are concerned with (the reminder is especially opportune) is an arrangement of words on the page and their effects—the emotions, attitudes, and ideas that they organize.

Our reaction, as Swift says, is not that of the butt or victim;

[3] *A Tale of a Tub*: the Preface.

nevertheless, it necessarily entails some measure of sympathetic self-projection. We more often, probably, feel the effect of the words as an intensity in the castigator than as an effect upon a victim: the dissociation of animus from the usual signs defines for our contemplation a peculiarly intense contempt or disgust. When, as sometimes we have to do, we talk in terms of effect on the victim, then "surprise" becomes an obviously apt word; he is to be betrayed, again and again, into an incipient acquiescence:

> *Sixthly,* This would be a great Inducement to Marriage, which all wise Nations have either encouraged by Rewards, or enforced by Laws and Penalties. It would increase the Care and Tenderness of Mothers towards their Children, when they were sure of a Settlement for Life, to the poor Babes, provided in some Sort by the Publick, to their annual Profit instead of Expence; we should soon see an honest Emulation among the married Women, *which of them could bring the fattest Child to the Market.* Men would become as *fond* of their Wives, during the Time of their Pregnancy, as they are now of their *Mares* in Foal, their *Cows* in Calf, or *Sows* when they are ready to farrow, nor offer to beat or kick them (as is too *frequent* a Practice) for fear of a Miscarriage.

The implication is: "This, as you so obligingly demonstrate, is the only kind of argument that appeals to you; here are your actual faith and morals. How, on consideration, do you like the smell of them?"

But when in reading the *Modest Proposal* we are most engaged, it is an effect directly upon ourselves that we are most disturbingly aware of. The dispassionate, matter-of-fact tone induces a feeling and a motion of assent, while the burden, at the same time, compels the feelings appropriate to rejection, and in the contrast—the tension—a remarkably disturbing energy is generated. A sense of an extraordinary energy is the general effect of Swift's irony. The intensive means just indicated are reinforced extensively in the continuous and unpredictable movement of the attack, which turns this way and that, comes now from one quarter and now from another, inexhaustibly surprising—making again an odd contrast with the sustained and level gravity of the tone. If Swift does for a moment appear to settle down to a formula it is only in order to betray; to induce a trust in the solid ground before opening the pitfall.

"His *Tale of a Tub* has little resemblance to his other pieces. It exhibits a vehemence and rapidity of mind, a copiousness of images, a vivacity of diction, such as he afterwards never possessed, or never exerted. It is of a mode so distinct and peculiar, that it must be considered by itself; what is true of that, is not true of anything else he has written."—What Johnson is really testifying to here is the degree in which the *Tale of a Tub* is characteristic and presents the qualities of Swift's genius in concentrated form. "That he has in his works no metaphors, as has been said, is not true," says Johnson a sentence or two later, "but his few metaphors seem to be received rather by necessity than choice." This last judgment may at any rate serve to enforce Johnson's earlier observation that in the *Tale of a Tub* Swift's powers function with unusual freedom. For the "copiousness of images" that Johnson constates is, as the phrase indicates, not a matter of choice but of essential genius. And, as a matter of fact, in this "copiousness of images" the characteristics that we noted in discussing Swift's pamphleteering irony have their supreme expression.

It is as if the gift applied in *Gulliver* to a very limiting task— directed and confined by a scheme uniting a certain consistency in analogical elaboration with verisimilitude—were here enjoying free play. For the bent expressing itself in this "copiousness" is clearly fundamental. It shows itself in the spontaneous metaphorical energy of Swift's prose—in the image, action, or blow that, leaping out of the prosaic manner, continually surprises and disconcerts the reader: "Such a man, truly wise, creams off Nature, leaving the sour and the dregs for philosophy and reason to lap up." It appears with as convincing a spontaneity in the sardonic vivacity of comic vision that characterizes the narrative, the presentment of action and actor. If, then, the continual elaborate play of analogy is a matter of cultivated habit, it is a matter also, of cultivated natural bent, a congenial development. It is a development that would seem to bear a relation to the Metaphysical fashion in verse (Swift was born in 1667). The spirit of it is that of a fierce and insolent game, but a game to which Swift devotes himself with a creative intensity.

And whereas the mind of man, when he gives the spur and bridle to his thoughts, does never stop, but naturally sallies out into both extremes of high and low, of good and evil, his first flight of fancy commonly transports him to ideas of what is most perfect, finished, and exalted, till, having soared out of his own reach and sight, not

well perceiving how near the frontiers of height and depth border
upon each other, with the same course and wing he falls down plump
into the lowest bottom of things, like one who travels the east into
the west, or like a straight line drawn by its own length into a circle.
Whether a tincture of malice in our natures makes us fond of furnishing every bright idea with its reverse, or whether reason, reflecting
upon the sum of things, can, like the sun, serve only to enlighten
one half of the globe, leaving the other half by necessity under shade
and darkness, or whether fancy, flying up to the imagination of what
is highest and best, becomes over-short, and spent, and weary, and
suddenly falls, like a dead bird of paradise, to the ground . . .

—One may (without difficulty) resist the temptation to make the
point by saying that this is poetry; one is still tempted to say that
the use to which so exuberant an energy is put is a poet's. "Exuberant" seems, no doubt, a paradoxical word to apply to an energy
used as Swift uses his; but the case is essentially one for paradoxical
descriptions.

In his use of negative materials—negative emotions and attitudes
—there is something that it is difficult not to call creative, though
the aim always is destructive. Not all the materials, of course, are
negative: the "bird of paradise" in the passage above is alive as well
as dead. Effects of this kind, often much more intense, are characteristic of the *Tale of a Tub*, where surprise and contrast operate in
modes that there is some point in calling poetic. "The most hetero-
geneous ideas are yoked by violence together"—and in the juxta-
position intensity is generated.

"Paracelsus brought a squadron of stink-pot-flingers from the
snowy mountains of Rhætia"—this (which comes actually from the
Battle of the Books) does not represent what I have in mind; it is
at once too simple and too little charged with animus. Swift's intensities are intensities of rejection and negation; his poetic juxta-
positions are, characteristically, destructive in intention, and when
they most seem creative of energy are most successful in spoiling,
reducing, and destroying. Sustained "copiousness," continually vary-
ing, and concentrating surprise in sudden local foci, cannot be represented in short extracts; it must suffice here to say that this kind
of thing may be found at a glance on almost any page:

Meantime it is my earnest request that so useful an undertaking
may be entered upon (if their Majesties please) with all convenient

speed, because I have a strong inclination before I leave the world to taste a blessing which we mysterious writers can seldom reach till we have got into our graves, whether it is that fame, being a fruit grafted on the body, can hardly grow and much less ripen till the stock is in the earth, or whether she be a bird of prey, and is lured among the rest to pursue after the scent of a carcass, or whether she conceives her trumpet sounds best and farthest when she stands on a tomb, by the advantage of a rising ground and the echo of a hollow vault.

It is, of course, possible to adduce Swift's authority for finding that his negations carry with them a complementary positive—an implicit assertion. But (*pace* Charles Whibley) the only thing in the nature of a positive that most readers will find convincingly present is self-assertion—*superbia*. Swift's way of demonstrating his superiori⁺y is to destroy, but he takes a positive delight in his power. And that the reader's sense of the negativeness of the *Tale of a Tub* is really qualified comes out when we refer to the Yahoos and the Struldbrugs for a test. The ironic detachment is of such a kind as to reassure us that this savage exhibition is mainly a game, played because it is the insolent pleasure of the author: "demonstration of superiority" is as good a formula as any for its prevailing spirit. Nevertheless, about a superiority that asserts itself in this way there is something disturbingly odd, and again and again in the *Tale of a Tub* we come on intensities that shift the stress decisively and remind us how different from Voltaire Swift is, even in his most complacent detachment.

I propose to examine in illustration a passage from the *Digression Concerning the Original, the Use, and Improvement of Madness in a Commonwealth (i.e.,* Section IX). It will have, in the nature of the case, to be a long one, but since it exemplifies at the same time all Swift's essential characteristics, its length will perhaps be tolerated. I shall break up the passage for convenience of comment, but, except for the omission of nine or ten lines in the second installment, quotation will be continuous:

For the brain in its natural position and state of serenity disposeth its owner to pass his life in the common forms, without any thought of subduing multitudes to his own power, his reasons, or his visions, and the more he shapes his understanding by the pattern of human learning, the less he is inclined to form parties after his particular

notions, because that instructs him in his private infirmities, as well
as in the stubborn ignorance of the people. But when a man's fancy
gets astride on his reason, when imagination is at cuffs with the senses,
and common understanding as well as common sense is kicked out of
doors, the first proselyte he makes is himself; and when that is once
compassed, the difficulty is not so great in bringing over others, a
strong delusion always operating from without as vigorously as from
within. For cant and vision are to the ear and the eye the same that
tickling is to the touch. Those entertainments and pleasures we most
value in life are such as dupe and play the wag with the senses. For
if we take an examination of what is generally understood by happiness, as it has respect either to the understanding or to the senses,
we shall find all its properties and adjuncts will herd under this short
definition, that it is a perpetual possession of being well deceived.

Swift's ant-like energy—the business-like air, obsessed intentness,
and unpredictable movement—have already had an effect. We are
not, at the end of this installment, as sure that we know just what
his irony is doing as we were at the opening. Satiric criticism of
sectarian "enthusiasm" by reference to the "common forms"—the
Augustan standards—is something that, in Swift, we can take as
very seriously meant. But in the incessant patter of the argument
we have (helped by such things as, at the end, the suggestion of
animus in that oddly concrete "herd") a sense that direction and
tone are changing. Nevertheless, the change of tone for which the
next passage is most remarkable comes as a disconcerting surprise:

And first, with relation to the mind or understanding, it is manifest
what mighty advantages fiction has over truth, and the reason is just
at our elbow; because imagination can build nobler scenes and produce more wonderful revolutions than fortune or Nature will be at
the expense to furnish. . . . Again, if we take this definition of happiness and examine it with reference to the senses, it will be acknowledged wonderfully adapt. How sad and insipid do all objects accost
us that are not conveyed in the vehicle of delusion! How shrunk is
everything as it appears in the glass of Nature, so that if it were not
for the assistance of artificial mediums, false lights, refracted angles,
varnish, and tinsel, there would be a mighty level in the felicity and
enjoyments of mortal men. If this were seriously considered by the
world, as I have a certain reason to suspect it hardly will, men would
no longer reckon among their high points of wisdom the art of exposing weak sides and publishing infirmities—an employment, in my

opinion, neither better nor worse than that of unmasking, which, I
think, has never been allowed fair usage, either in the world or the
playhouse.

The suggestion of changing direction does not, in the first part of
this passage, bring with it anything unsettling: from ridicule of
"enthusiasm" to ridicule of human capacity for self-deception is
an easy transition. The reader, as a matter of fact, begins to settle
down to the habit, the steady drift of this irony, and is completely
unprepared for the sudden change of tone and reversal of attitude
in the two sentences beginning: "How sad and insipid do all objects," etc. Exactly what the change means or is, it is difficult to be
certain (and that is of the essence of the effect). But the tone has
certainly a personal intensity and the ironic detachment seems
suddenly to disappear. It is as if one found Swift in the place—
at the point of view—where one expected to find his butt. But the
ambiguously mocking sentence with which the paragraph ends re-
inforces the uncertainty.

The next paragraph keeps the reader for some time in uneasy
doubt. The irony has clearly shifted its plane, but in which direction is the attack going to develop? Which, to be safe, must one
dissociate oneself from, "credulity" or "curiosity"?

In the proportion that credulity is a more peaceful possession of the
mind than curiosity, so far preferable is that wisdom which converses
about the surface to that pretended philosophy which enters into the
depths of things and then comes gravely back with informations and
discoveries, that in the inside they are good for nothing. The two
senses to which all objects first address themselves are the sight and
the touch; these never examine further than the colour, the shape,
the size, and whatever other qualities dwell or are drawn by art upon
the outward of bodies; and then comes reason officiously, with tools
for cutting, and opening, and mangling, and piercing, offering to
demonstrate that they are not of the same consistence quite through.
Now I take all this to be the last degree of perverting Nature, one
of whose eternal laws is to put her best furniture forward. And therefore, in order to save the charges of all such expensive anatomy for
the time to come, I do here think fit to inform the reader that in
such conclusions as these reason is certainly in the right; and that in
most corporeal beings which have fallen under my cognisance the
outside hath been infinitely preferable to the in, whereof I have been
further convinced from some late experiments. Last week I saw a

woman flayed, and you will hardly believe how much it altered her person for the worse.

The peculiar intensity of that last sentence is, in its own way, so decisive that it has for the reader the effect of resolving uncertainty in general. The disturbing force of the sentence is a notable instance of a kind already touched on: repulsion is intensified by the momentary co-presence, induced by the tone, of incipient and incompatible feelings (or motions) of acceptance. And that Swift feels the strongest animus against "curiosity" is now beyond all doubt. The natural corollary would seem to be that "credulity," standing ironically for the "common forms"—the sane, socially sustained, common-sense illusions—is the positive that the reader must associate himself with and rest on for safety. The next half-page steadily and (to all appearances) unequivocally confirms this assumption:

> Yesterday I ordered the carcass of a beau to be stripped in my presence, when we were all amazed to find so many unsuspected faults under one suit of clothes. Then I laid open his brain, his heart, and his spleen, but I plainly perceived at every operation that the farther we proceeded, we found the defects increase upon us in number and bulk; from all of which I justly formed this conclusion to myself, that whatever philosopher or projector can find out an art to sodder and patch up the flaws and imperfections of Nature, will deserve much better of mankind and teach us a much more useful science than that, so much in present esteem, of widening and exposing them (like him who held anatomy to be the ultimate end of physic). And he whose fortunes and dispositions have placed him in a convenient station to enjoy the fruits of this noble art, he that can with Epicurus content his ideas with the films and images that fly off upon his senses from the superficies of things, such a man, truly wise, creams off Nature, leaving the sour and the dregs for philosophy and reason to lap up.

Assumption has become habit, and has been so nourished that few readers note anything equivocal to trouble them in that last sentence: the concrete force of "creams off," "sour," "dregs," and "lap up" seems unmistakably to identify Swift with an intense animus against "philosophy and reason" (understood implicitly to stand for "curiosity" the anatomist). The reader's place, of course, is with Swift.

The trap is sprung in the last sentence of the paragraph:

> This is the sublime and refined point of felicity called the possession of being well-deceived, the serene peaceful state of being a fool among knaves.

What is left? The next paragraph begins significantly: "But to return to madness." This irony may be critical, but "critical" turns out, in no very long run, to be indistinguishable from "negative." The positives disappear. Even when, as in the Houyhnhnms, they seem to be more substantially present, they disappear under our "curiosity." The Houyhnhnms, of course, stand for Reason, Truth, and Nature, the Augustan positives, and it was in deadly earnest that Swift appealed to these; but how little at best they were anything solidly realized comparison with Pope brings out. Swift did his best for the Houyhnhnms, and they may have all the reason, but the Yahoos have all the life. Gulliver's master "thought Nature and reason were sufficient guides for a reasonable animal," but nature and reason as Gulliver exhibits them are curiously negative, and the reasonable animals appear to have nothing in them to guide. "They have no fondness for their colts or foals, but the care they take in educating them proceeds entirely from the dictates of reason." This freedom from irrational feelings and impulses simplifies other matters too: "Their language doth not abound in variety of words, because their wants and passions are fewer than among us." And so conversation, in this model society, is simplified: "nothing passed but what was useful, expressed in the fewest and most significant words . . ." "Courtship, love, presents, jointures, settlements, have no place in their thoughts, or terms whereby to express them in their language. The young couple meet and are joined, merely because it is the determination of their parents and friends: it is what they see done every day, and they look upon it as one of the necessary actions of a reasonable being." The injunction of "temperance, industry, exercise, and cleanliness . . . the lessons enjoined to the young ones of both sexes," seems unnecessary; except possibly for exercise, the usefulness of which would not, perhaps, be immediately apparent to the reasonably young.

The clean skin of the Houyhnhnms, in short, is stretched over a void; instincts, emotions, and life, which complicate the problem of

:leanliness and decency, are left for the Yahoos with the dirt and he indecorum. Reason, Truth, and Nature serve instead; the Houyhnhnms (who scorn metaphysics) find them adequate. Swift oo scorned metaphysics, and never found anything better to con-end for than a skin, a surface, an outward show. An outward show s, explicitly, all he contends for in the quite unironical *Project for the Advancement of Religion,* and the difference between the reality of religion and the show is, for the author of the *Tale of a Tub,* hardly substantial. Of Jack we are told, "nor could all the world persuade him, as the common phrase is, to eat his victuals like a Christian." It is characteristic of Swift that he should put in these terms, showing a complete incapacity even to guess what religious feeling might be, a genuine conviction that Jack should be made to kneel when receiving the Sacrament.

Of the intensity of this conviction there can be no doubt. The Church of England was the established "common form," and, more-over, was Swift's church: his insane egotism reinforced the savagery with which he fought to maintain this cover over the void, this decent surface. But what the savagery of the passage from the *Digression* shows mainly is Swift's sense of insecurity and of the un-disguisable flimsiness of any surface that offered.

The case, of course, is more complex. In the passage examined the "surface" becomes at the most savage moment, a human skin. Swift's negative horror, at its most disturbing, becomes one with his disgust-obsession: he cannot bear to be reminded that under the skin there is blood, mess, and entrails; and the skin itself, as we know from *Gulliver,* must not be seen from too close. Hypertrophy of the sense of uncleanness, of the instinct of repulsion, is not un-common; nor is its association with what accompanies it in Swift. What is uncommon is Swift's genius, and the paradoxical vitality with which this self-defeat of life—life turned against itself—is manifested. In the *Tale of a Tub* the defeat is also a triumph; the genius delights in its mastery, in its power to destroy, and negation is felt as self-assertion. It is only when time has confirmed Swift in disappointment and brought him to more intimate contemplation of physical decay that we get the Yahoos and the Struldbrugs.

Here, well on this side of pathology, literary criticism stops. To attempt encroachments would be absurd, and, even if one were qualified, unprofitable. No doubt psychopathology and medicine have an interesting commentary to offer, but their help is not necessary. Swift's genius belongs to literature, and its appreciation to literary criticism.

We have, then, in his writings probably the most remarkable expression of negative feelings and attitudes that literature can offer —the spectacle of creative powers (the paradoxical description seems right) exhibited consistently in negation and rejection. His verse demands an essay to itself, but fits in readily with what has been said. "In poetry," he reports of the Houyhnhnms, "they must be allowed to excel all other mortals; wherein the justness of their similes and the minuteness as well as exactness of their descriptions are, indeed, inimitable. Their verses abound very much in both of these. . . ." The actuality of presentment for which Swift is notable, in prose as well as verse, seems always to owe its convincing "justness" to, at his least actively malicious, a coldly intense scrutiny, a potentially hostile attention. "To his domesticks," says Johnson, "he was naturally rough; and a man of rigorous temper, with that vigilance of minute attention which his works discover, must have been a master that few could bear." *Instructions to Servants* and the *Polite Conversation* enforce obviously the critical bearing and felicity of Johnson's remark.

A great writer—yes; that account still imposes itself as fitting, though his greatness is no matter of moral grandeur or human centrality; our sense of it is merely a sense of great force. And this force, as we feel it, is conditioned by frustration and constriction; the channels of life have been blocked and perverted. That we should be so often invited to regard him as a moralist and an idealist would seem to be mainly a witness to the power of vanity, and the part that vanity can play in literary appreciation; *saeva indignatio* is an indulgence that solicits us all, and the use of literature by readers and critics for the projection of nobly suffering selves is familiar. No doubt, too, it is pleasant to believe that unusual capacity for egotistic animus means unusual distinction of intellect; but, as we have seen, there is no reason to lay stress on intellect in Swift. His work does indeed exhibit an extraordinary play of mind; but it is not great intellectual force that is exhibited in his indifference to the problems raised—in, for instance, the *Voyage to the Houyhnhnms*—by his use of the concept, or the word, "Nature." It is not merely that he had an Augustan contempt for metaphysics;

e shared the shallowest complacencies of Augustan common sense: is irony might destroy these, but there is no conscious criticism.

He was, in various ways, curiously unaware—the reverse of clair-oyant. He is distinguished by the intensity of his feelings, not by insight into them, and he certainly does not impress us as a mind n possession of its experience.

We shall not find Swift remarkable for intelligence if we think f Blake.

The Excremental Vision

by Norman O. Brown

Any reader of Jonathan Swift knows that in his analysis of human nature there is an emphasis on, and attitude toward, the anal function that is unique in Western literature. In mere quantity of scatological imagery he may be equaled by Rabelais and Aristophanes; but whereas for Rabelais and Aristophanes the anal function is a part of the total human being which they make us love because it is part of life, for Swift it becomes the decisive weapon in his assault on the pretensions, the pride, even the self-respect of mankind. The most scandalous pieces of Swiftian scatology are three of his later poems—*The Lady's Dressing Room, Strephon and Chloe, Cassinus and Peter*—which are all variations on the theme:

> Oh! *Caelia, Caelia, Caelia* ——.

Aldous Huxley explicates, saying, "The monosyllabic verb, which the modesties of 1929 will not allow me to reprint, rhymes with 'wits' and 'fits.' " [1] But even more disturbing, because more comprehensively metaphysical, is Swift's vision of man as Yahoo, and Yahoo as excrementally filthy beyond all other animals, in the fourth part of *Gulliver's Travels*. Nor is the anal theme a new feature in Swift's mature or later period; it is already adumbrated in *A Tale of a Tub*, that intoxicated overflow of youthful genius and fountainhead of the entire Swiftian apocalypse. The understanding of Swift therefore begins with the recognition that Swift's

[1] Huxley, *Do What You Will*, p. 94.

anatomy of human nature, in its entirety and at the most profound
and profoundly disturbing level, can be called "The Excremental
Vision."

"The Excremental Vision" is the title of a chapter in Middleton
Murry's book (1954) on Jonathan Swift.[2] The credit for recognizing
the central importance of the excremental theme in Swift belongs
to Aldous Huxley. In an essay in *Do What You Will* (1929) he says,
"Swift's greatness lies in the intensity, the almost insane violence of
that 'hatred of the bowels' which is the essence of his misanthropy
and which underlies the whole of his work."[3] Murry deserves credit
for his arresting phrase, which redirects criticism to the central
problem in Swift. Aldous Huxley's essay had no effect on Quintana's
book *The Mind and Art of Jonathan Swift* (1936), which perfectly
illustrates the poverty of criticism designed to domesticate and
housebreak this tiger of English literature. Quintana buries what
he calls the "noxious compositions" in a general discussion of Swift's
last phase as a writer, saying, "From scatology one turns with relief
to the capital verses entitled *Helter Skelter, or The Hue and Cry
after the Attorneys going to ride the Circuit,* which exhibits Swift's
complete mastery of vigorous rhythm." The excremental theme in
the fourth part of *Gulliver's Travels* is dismissed as bad art (criticism
here, as so often, functioning as a mask for moral prejudice): "The
sensationalism into which Swift falls while developing the theme of
bestiality. . . . Had part IV been toned down, *Gulliver's Travels*
would have been a finer work of art."[4] It is reassuring to know that
English literature is expounded at our leading universities by men
who, like Bowdler, know how to improve the classics. The history
of Swiftian criticism, like the history of psychoanalysis, shows that
repression weighs more heavily on anality than on genitality. Psychoanalytical theorems on the genital function have become legiti-
mate hypotheses in circles which will not listen to what Freud has
to say about anality, or to what Swift had to say (and who yet write
books on *The Mind and Art of Jonathan Swift*).

Even Huxley and Murry, though they face the problem, prove incapable of seeing what there is to see. After admitting into consciousness the unpleasant facts which previous criticism had repressed, they proceed to protect themselves and us against the

---

[2] Murry, *Jonathan Swift,* pp. 432-48.
[3] Huxley, *op. cit.,* p. 99.
[4] Quintana, *The Mind and Art of Jonathan Swift,* pp. 327, 360.

disturbing impact of the excremental vision by systematic distortion, denunciation, and depreciation. It is a perfect example, in the field of literary criticism, of Freud's notion that the first way in which consciousness becomes conscious of a repressed idea is by emphatically denying it.[5] The basic device for repudiating the excremental vision is, of course, denunciation. Huxley adopts a stance of intellectual superiority—"the absurdity, the childish silliness, of this refusal to accept the universe as it is given." [6] Murry, echoing that paradoxically conservative philosopher of sexuality, D. H. Lawrence, adopts a stance of moral superiority—"so perverse, so unnatural, so mentally diseased, so humanly *wrong*." [7] The transparently emotional character of their reaction to Swift is then masked as a psychoanalytical diagnosis; the excremental vision is a product of insanity. Huxley speaks of the "obsessive preoccupation with the visceral and excrementitious subject, . . . to the verge of insanity," and suggests a connection between it and the "temperamental coldness" of Swift's relations to Stella and Vanessa, implying a disturbance in the genital function.[8]

Murry's attempt to transform Huxley's suggestions into a full-dress biography is a case study in perverted argumentation. The texts of the "noxious compositions" and the fourth part of *Gulliver* are crudely distorted, as we shall see later, so as to transform Swift's misanthropy into misogyny; then the entire excremental vision can be explained away as an attempt to justify his genital failure (with Varina, Vanessa, and Stella) by indicting the filthiness of the female sex. It is falsely insinuated that the excremental vision is restricted to Swift's latest phase. This insinuation not only has the advantage of suggesting that there is a Swiftian vision which is not excremental (on this point Huxley is more tough-minded than Murry); it has the further advantage of linking the excremental vision with Swift's final mental breakdown. The fact that the mental breakdown came ten years later (1742) will not stop anyone ignorant of psychopathology and determined to lobotomize Swift's scatology; the chronological gap is filled by an enthusiastic vision of Swift's mental breakdown as God's punishment for the scatology. The fact that the

---

[5] *Collected Papers*, ed. J. Rivière and J. Strachey (New York and London, 1924-50), V, 182.

[6] Huxley, *op. cit.*, p. 101.

[7] Murry, *op. cit.*, p. 440; Lawrence, *Sex, Literature and Censorship*, p. 60.

[8] Huxley, *op. cit.*, pp. 94, 104.

excremental theme is already prominent in the fourth part of
Gulliver (1723) is explained away by a little psychoanalytical jargon
buttressed by a little flight of historical imagination: "Evidently
the whole complex was working in Swift's mind when he wrote the
fourth part of *Gulliver*. . . . Its emergence at that moment may
have been the outcome of a deep emotional upheaval caused by the
death of Vanessa." The prominence of the same complex in the
Letter of Advice to a Young Poet (1721), two years before the death
of Vanessa, is ignored. Murry's amateur diagnosis finds the origin
of the entire complex in Swift's rejection by Varina (1696). It is
therefore essential to his thesis to regard *A Tale of a Tub* (1696-
1698) as uninfected by the complex. Murry sustains this interpretation by averting his eyes from the prominence of anality in the
Tale and by interpreting the whole book as wonderful tomfoolery
which is not to be taken seriously—that is, by a notion of comedy
which denies meaning to wit.[9]

If the duty of criticism toward Jonathan Swift is to judge him
insane, criticism should be turned over to the psychoanalysts. They
have risen to the occasion and have shown that they can be counted
on to issue a medical certificate of insanity against genius. Their
general verdict is substantially the same as that of Huxley and
Murry, with the addition of some handsome new terminology. Thus
Ferenczi (1926): "From the psychoanalytical standpoint one would
describe his neurotic behaviour as an inhibition of normal potency,
with a lack of courage in relation to women of good character and
perhaps with a lasting aggressive tendency towards women of a
lower type. This insight into Swift's life surely justifies us who come
after him in treating the phantasies in *Gulliver's Travels* exactly as
we do the free associations of neurotic patients in analysis, especially
when interpreting their dreams." [10] Karpman (1942): "It is submit-
ted on the basis of such a study of *Gulliver's Travels* that Swift was
a neurotic who exhibited psychosexual infantilism, with a particular
showing of coprophilia, associated with misogyny, misanthropy,
mysophilia and mysophobia." [11] Greenacre (1955): "One gets the
impression that the anal fixation was intense and binding, and the
genital demands so impaired or limited at best that there was a total

---

[9] Murry, *op. cit.*, pp. 78-82, 86, 346-55, 432-48.
[10] Ferenczi, *Final Contributions*, p. 59.
[11] Karpman, "Neurotic Traits of Jonathan Swift," p. 132.

retreat from genital sexuality in his early adult life, probably beginning with the unhappy relationship with Jane Waring, the first of the goddesses." [12]

In developing their diagnosis, the psychoanalysts, as might be expected, trace the origin of Swift's neurosis to his earliest childhood. If the psychoanalytical theory of the neuroses is correct, we must abandon Murry's attempt to isolate the excremental vision as a late excrescence; we must also abandon Murry's thesis (interconnected with his attempt to salvage part of Swift for respectability) that until he was rejected by her, Swift's love for Varina (Jane Waring) was "the healthy natural love of a naturally passionate, and naturally generous nature." [13] We shall have to return to Huxley's more tough-minded literary judgment that Swift *is* the excremental vision, and to his more tough-minded psychological judgment that Swift's sexuality was structurally abnormal from the start. And the biographical evidence, most carefully analyzed by Greenacre, supplies more than enough confirmation. Swift lost his father before he was born; was kidnaped from his mother by his nurse at the age of one; was returned to his mother only three years later, only to be abandoned by his mother one month after his return to her at the psychoanalytically crucial Oedipal period.[14] By psychoanalytical standards such a succession of infantile traumata must establish more than a predisposition to lifelong neurosis.

The case, then, would appear to be closed. The psychoanalytical experts concur with the critics that Swift was mad and that his works should be read only as documents in a case history. Not just the fourth part of *Gulliver* and the "noxious compositions" but all of Swift. For if we cry "insane" to the objectionable parts of Swift, in all honesty we must hand the case over to the psychoanalysts. But after psychoanalytical scrutiny, there is nothing left of Swift that is not objectionable. We must not understimate the ability of psychoanalysis to uncover the real meaning of symbols. For example, a psychoanalytical comment on Gulliver as a little man in a little boat on the island of Brobdingnag says that "the common symbolism of the man in the boat as the clitoris suggests the identification

---

[12] Greenacre, "The Mutual Adventures of Jonathan Swift and Lemuel Gulliver," p. 60.

[13] Murry, *op. cit.*, p. 60.

[14] Greenacre, *op. cit.*, pp. 21-22.

with the female phallus thought to be characteristic of the male transvestite." Similarly, psychoanalysis leaves the Dean's character without a shred of integrity. "Swift showed marked anal characteristics (his extreme personal immaculateness, secretiveness, intense ambition, pleasure in less obvious dirt [sc. satire], stubborn vengefulness in righteous causes) which indicate clearly that early control of the excretory function was achieved under great stress and perhaps too early." [15]

At this point common humanity revolts. If personal immaculateness, ambition, and the championship of righteous causes are neurotic traits, who shall 'scape whipping? And certainly no genius will escape if this kind of psychoanalysis is turned loose on literary texts. Common humanity makes us turn in revulsion against Huxley, Murry, and the psychoanalysts. By what right do they issue certificates of lunacy? By virtue of their own pre-eminent sanity? Judged for sanity and truthfulness, *Gulliver's Travels* will not suffer in comparison with the works of Murry and Huxley. Only Swift could do justice to the irony of Huxley condemning Swift for misanthropic distortion in a volume of essays devoted to destroying the integrity not only of Swift, but also of St. Francis and Pascal. Nor is the sanity of psychoanalysts—and their interpretations of what a man in a boat signifies—utterly beyond question. Only Swift could do justice to the irony of psychoanalysts, whose capacity for finding the anus in the most unlikely places is notorious, condemning Swift for obsessive preoccupation with anality. Fortunately Swift is not himself speechless in the face of these accusations of insanity:

> He gave the little Wealth he had
> To build a House for Fools and Mad.[16]

In Dr. Swift's mental hospital there is a room for Huxley and Murry; their religious eccentricities are prefigured under the name of Jack, the prototype of religious enthusiasm in *A Tale of a Tub*. For Huxley, as for Jack, it later came to pass that "it was for certain reported that he had run out of his Wits. In a short time after, he appeared abroad, and confirmed the Report by falling into the odd-

---

[15] Greenacre, *op. cit.*, pp. 41, 56.
[16] Swift, *Verses on the Death of Dr. Swift*, vss. 479-80.

est Whimsies that ever a sick Brain conceived." [17] Swift has also prepared a room for the psychoanalysts with their anal complex; for are they not prophetically announced as those "certain Fortune-tellers in Northern America, who have a Way of reading a Man's Destiny, by peeping in his Breech"? [18]

The argument thus ends in a bedlamite babel filling the air with mutual accusations of madness. If we resist the temptation to stop our ears and run away, if we retain a psychiatric interest and a clinical detachment, we can only conclude that the accusations are all justified; they are all mad. And the crux of their madness is their proud insistence that everybody except themselves —Huxley, Murry, the psychoanalysts—are mad. We can only save ourselves from their madness by admitting that we are all mad. Psychoanalysis deserves the severest strictures, because it should have helped mankind to develop this kind of consciousness and this kind of humility. Freud saw psychoanalysis as the third great wound, comparable to the Newtonian and Darwinian revolutions, inflicted by science on human narcissism.[19] The Epigoni of Freud have set themselves up as a proud elect exempt from the general damnation. As we have argued elsewhere, the proper aim of psychoanalysis is the diagnosis of the universal neurosis of mankind, in which psychoanalysis is itself a symptom and a stage, like any other phase in the intellectual history of mankind.

If we reorient psychoanalysis in this direction, then a different method for the application of psychoanalysis to Swift (or any other literary figure) is in order. We no longer try to explain away Swift's literary achievements as mere epiphenomena on his individual neurosis. Rather we seek to appreciate his insight into the universal neurosis of mankind. Then psychoanalysis becomes a method not for explaining away but for explicating Swift. We are not disturbed by the fact that Swift had his individual version of the universal human neurosis; we are not even disturbed by the thought that his individual neurosis may have been abnormally acute, or by the thought that his abnormality may be inseparable from his art.

[17] Swift, *A Tale of a Tub*, in *Prose Works of Jonathan Swift* (Oxford, 1939), I, 88.

[18] Swift, *A Discourse Concerning the Mechanical Operation of the Spirit, Etc.*, in *Prose Works of Jonathan Swift* (Oxford, 1939), I, 186.

[19] CP IV, 351-55.

Intense suffering may be necessary, though not sufficient, for the production of genius; and psychoanalysis has never thought through its position towards the age-old tradition of an affinity between genius and madness. Perhaps there is that "necessity of doctors and nurses *who themselves are sick*" of which Nietzsche spoke.[20] Psychoanalysis is then not less necessary for the study of Swift, but more so, though in a different way. It is necessary in order to sustain the requisite posture of humility—about ourselves, about mankind, and toward genius. It is also necessary in order to take seriously the Swiftian exploration of the universal neurosis of mankind. The thesis of this chapter is that if we are willing to listen to Swift we will find startling anticipations of Freudian theorems about anality, about sublimation, and about the universal neurosis of mankind. To anticipate objections, let me say that Swiftian psychoanalysis differs from the Freudian in that the vehicle for the exploration of the unconscious is not psychoanalysis but wit. But Freud himself recognized, in *Wit and the Unconscious*, that wit has its own way of exploring the universal neurosis of mankind.

Psychoanalysis is apparently necessary in order to explicate the "noxious compositions"; at least the unpsychoanalyzed neurotic appears to be incapable of correctly stating what these poems are about. These are the poems which provoke Murry to ecstasies of revulsion—"nonsensical and intolerable," "so perverse, so unnatural, so mentally diseased, so humanly *wrong.*" What Murry is denouncing is the proposition that woman is abominable because she is guilty of physical evacuation. We need not consider whether the proposition deserves such denunciation, for the simple reason that it comes from Murry's imagination, not Swift's. Murry, like Strephon and the other unfortunate men in the poems, loses his wits when he discovers that Caelia ----, and thus unconsciously bears witness to the truth of Swift's psychological insight. Any mind that is at all open to the antiseptic wisdom of psychoanalysis will find nothing extraordinary about the poems, except perhaps the fact that they were written in the first half of the eighteenth century. For their real theme—quite obvious on a dispassionate reading—is the conflict between our animal body, appropriately epitomized in the anal function, and our pretentious sublimations,

[20] Nietzsche, *The Philosophy of Nietzsche*, p. 752.

more specifically the pretensions of sublimated or romantic-Platonic love. In every case it is a "goddess," "so divine a Creature," "heavenly Chloe," who is exposed; or rather what is exposed is the illusion in the head of the adoring male, the illusion that the goddess is all head and wings, with no bottom to betray her sublunary infirmities.

The peculiar Swiftian twist to the theme that Caelia ------ is the notion that there is some absolute contradition between the state of being in love and an awareness of the excremental function of the beloved. Before we dismiss this idea as the fantasy of a diseased mind, we had better remember that Freud said the same thing. In an essay written in 1912 surveying the disorder in the sexual life of man, he finally concludes that the deepest trouble is an unresolved ambivalence in the human attitude toward anality:[21]

> We know that at its beginning the sexual instinct is divided into a large number of components—or rather it develops from them—not all of which can be carried on into its final form; some have to be surpassed or turned to other uses before the final form results. Above all, the coprophilic elements in the instinct have proved incompatible with our aesthetic ideas, probably since the time when man developed an upright posture and so removed his organ of smell from the ground; further, a considerable proportion of the sadistic elements belonging to the erotic instinct have to be abandoned. All such developmental processes, however, relate only to the upper layers of the complicated structure. The fundamental processes which promote erotic excitation remain always the same. Excremental things are all too intimately and inseparably bound up with sexual things; the position of the genital organs—*inter urinas et faeces*—remain the decisive and unchangeable factor. The genitals themselves have not undergone the development of the rest of the human form in the direction of beauty; they have retained their animal cast; and so even today love, too, is in essence as animal as it ever was.

Again, in *Civilization and Its Discontents,* Freud pursues the thought that the deepest cause of sexual repression is an organic factor, a disbalance in the human organism between higher and lower functions:[22]

[21] CP IV, 215.
[22] Freud, *Civilization and Its Discontents,* 78n.

The whole of sexuality and not merely anal erotism is threatened with falling a victim to the organic repression consequent upon man's adoption of the erect posture and the lowering in value of the sense of smell; so that since that time the sexual function has been associated with a resistance not susceptible of further explanation, which puts obstacles in the way of full satisfaction and forces it away from its sexual aim towards sublimations and displacements of libido. . . . All neurotics, and many others too, take exception to the fact that *"inter urinas et faeces nascimur."* . . . Thus we should find, as the deepest root of the sexual repression that marches with culture, the organic defense of the new form of life that began with the erect posture.

Those who, like Middleton Murry, anathematize Swift's excremental vision as unchristian might ponder the quotation from St. Augustine that Freud uses in both these passages.

That Swift's thought is running parallel with Freud's is demonstrated by the fact that a fuller explication of the poems would have to use the terms "repression" and "sublimation." It is of course not ignorance but repression of the anal factor that creates the romantic illusions of Strephon and Cassinus and makes the breakthrough of the truth so traumatic. And Swift's ultimate horror in these poems is at the thought that sublimation—that is to say, all civilized behavior—is a lie and cannot survive confrontation with the truth. In the first of his treatments of the theme (*The Lady's Dressing Room,* 1730) he reasons with Strephon that sublimation is still possible:

> Should I the Queen of Love refuse,
> Because she rose from stinking Ooze?

Strephon should reconcile himself to—

> Such Order from Confusion sprung,
> Such gaudy Tulips rais'd from Dung.

But in *Strephon and Chloe* (1731) sublimation and awareness of the excremental function are presented as mutually exclusive, and the conclusion is drawn that sublimation must be cultivated at all costs, even at the cost of repression:

Authorities both old and recent
Direct that Women must be decent:
And, from the Spouse each Blemish hide
More than from all the World beside . . .
On Sense and Wit your Passion found,
By Decency cemented round.

In *Cassinus and Peter,* the last of these poems, even this solution
is exploded. The life of civilized sublimation, epitomized in the
word "wit," is shattered because the excremental vision cannot be
repressed. The poem tells of two undergraduates—

Two College Sophs of *Cambridge* growth
Both special Wits, and Lovers both—

and Cassinus explains the trauma which is killing him:

Nor wonder how I lost my Wits;
Oh! *Caelia, Caelia, Caelia* sh—.

That blessed race of horses, the Houyhnhnms, are free from
the illusions of romantic-Platonic love, or rather they are free from
love. "Courtship, Love, Presents, Joyntures, Settlements, have no
place in their thoughts; or Terms whereby to express them in their
Language. The young Couple meet and are joined, merely because
it is the Determination of their Parents and Friends: it is what
they see done every Day; and they look upon it as one of the
necessary Actions in a reasonable Being." [23] If the Houyhnhnms
represent a critique of the genital function and genital institutions
of mankind, the Yahoos represent a critique of the anal function.

The Yahoos represent the raw core of human bestiality; but the
essence of Swift's vision and Gulliver's redemption is the recog-
nition that the civilized man of Western Europe not only remains
Yahoo but is worse than Yahoo—"a sort of Animals to whose
Share, by what Accident he could not conjecture, some small
Pittance of *Reason* had fallen, whereof we made no other use

───

[23] Swift, *Gulliver's Travels,* in *Prose Works of Jonathan Swift* (Oxford, 1941),
XI, 253.

than by its Assistance to aggravate our *natural* Corruptions, and to acquire new ones which Nature had not given us." And the essence of the Yahoo is filthiness, a filthiness distinguishing them not from Western European man but from all other animals: "Another Thing he wondered at in the *Yahoos,* was their strange Disposition to Nastiness and Dirt; whereas there appears to be a natural Love of Cleanliness in all other Animals." The Yahoo is physically endowed with a very rank smell—"the Stink was somewhat between a *Weasel* and a *Fox*"—which, heightened at mating time, is a positive attraction to the male of the species. The recognition of the rank odor of humanity stays with Gulliver after his return to England: "During the first Year I could not endure my Wife or Children in my Presence, the very Smell of them was intolerable"; when he walked the street, he kept his nose "well stopt with Rue, Lavender, or Tobacco-leaves." The Yahoo eating habits are equally filthy: "There was nothing that rendered the *Yahoos* more odious, than their undistinguishing Appetite to devour everything that came in their Way, whether Herbs, Roots, Berries, corrupted Flesh of Animals, or all mingled together."

But above all the Yahoos are distinguished from other animals by their attitude toward their own excrement. Excrement to the Yahoos is no mere waste product but a magic instrument for self-expression and aggression. This attitude begins in infancy: "While I held the odious Vermin in my Hands, it voided its filthy Excrements of a yellow liquid Substance, all over my Cloaths." It continues in adulthood: "Several of this cursed Brood getting hold of the Branches behind, leaped up into the Tree, from whence they began to discharge their Excrements on my Head." It is part of the Yahoo ritual symbolizing the renewal of society: when the old leader of the herd is discarded, "his Successor, at the Head of all the *Yahoos* in that District, Young and Old, Male and Female, come in a Body, and discharge their Excrements upon him from Head to Foot." Consequently, in the Yahoo system of social infeudation, "this *Leader* had usually a Favourite as *like himself* as he could get, whose Employment was to *lick his Master's Feet and Posteriors, and drive the Female* Yahoos *to his Kennel.*" This recognition that the human animal is distinguished from others as the distinctively excremental animal stays with Gulliver after his return to England, so that he finds relief from the oppressive smell of mankind in the company of his groom: "For I feel my

Spirits revived by the Smell he contracts in the Stable." Swift does not, as Huxley says he does, hate the bowels, but only the human use of the bowels.[24]

This demonic presentation of the excremental nature of humanity is the great stumbling block in *Gulliver's Travels*—an aesthetic lapse, crude sensationalism, says Quintana; a false libel on humanity, says Middleton Murry, "for even if we carry the process of stripping the human to the limit of imaginative possibility, we do not arrive at the Yahoo. We might arrive at his cruelty and malice; we should never arrive at his nastiness and filth. That is a gratuitous degradation of humanity; not a salutary, but a shocking one." [25] But if we measure Swift's correctness not by the conventional and complacent prejudices in favor of human pride which are back of Quintana's and Murry's strictures, but by the ruthless wisdom of psychoanalysis, then it is quite obvious that the excremental vision of the Yahoo is substantially identical with the psychoanalytical doctrine of the extensive role of anal erotism in the formation of human culture.

According to Freudian theory the human infant passes through a stage—the anal stage—as a result of which the libido, the life energy of the body, gets concentrated in the anal zone. This infantile stage of anal erotism takes the essential form of attaching symbolic meaning to the anal product. As a result of these symbolic equations the anal product acquires for the child the significance of being his own child or creation, which he may use either to obtain narcissistic pleasure in play, or to obtain love from another (feces as gift), or to assert independence from another (feces as property), or to commit aggression against another (feces as weapon). Thus some of the most important categories of social behavior (play, gift, property, weapon) originate in the anal stage of infantile sexuality and—what is more important—never lose their connection with it. When infantile sexuality comes to its catastrophic end, nonbodily cultural objects inherit the symbolism originally attached to the anal product, but only as second-best substitutes for the original (sublimations). Sublimations are thus symbols of symbols. The category of property is not simply transferred from feces to money; on the contrary, money is feces,

[24] *Gulliver's Travels*, pp. 243, 245-47, 250, 272-74.
[25] Murry, *op. cit.*, p. 352; Quintana, *op. cit.*, p. 327.

because the anal erotism continues in the unconscious. The anal erotism has not been renounced or abandoned but repressed.[26]

One of the central ambiguities in psychoanalytical theory is the question of whether the pregenital infantile organizations of the libido, including the anal organization, are biologically determined. We have elsewhere taken the position that they are not biologically determined but are constructed by the human ego, or rather that they represent that distortion of the human body which *is* the human ego. If so, then psychoanalysis concurs with Swift's thesis that anal erotism—in Swift's language, "a strange Disposition to Nastiness and Dirt"—is a specifically human privilege; on the other hand, psychoanalysis would differ from Swift's implication that the strange Disposition to Nastiness and Dirt is biologically given. It comes to the same thing to say that Swift errs in giving the Yahoos no "Pittance of Reason" and in assigning to Reason only the transformation of the Yahoo into the civilized man of Western Europe. If anal organization is constructed by the human ego, then the strange Disposition to Nastiness and Dirt is a primal or infantile manifestation of human Reason. Swift also antici- pates Freud in emphasizing the connection between anal erotism and human aggression. The Yahoos' filthiness is manifested pri- marily in excremental aggression: psychoanalytical theory stresses the interconnection between anal organization and human ag- gression to the point of labeling this phase of infantile sexuality the anal-sadistic phase. Defiance, mastery, will to power are at- tributes of human reason first developed in the symbolic manipula- tion of excrement and perpetuated in the symbolic manipulation of symbolic substitutes for excrement.

The psychoanalytical theory of anal erotism depends on the psychoanalytical theory of sublimation. If money etc. are not feces, there is not much reason for hypothesizing a strange human fasci- nation with excrement. By the same token it is hard to see how Swift could have come by his anticipation of the doctrine of sublimation. But Swift did anticipate the doctrine of sublimation. Full credit for perceiving this goes to William Empson. Referring to *A Tale of a Tub* and its appendix, *The Mechanical Operation of the Spirit,* Empson writes:[27]

[26] Cf. CP II, 45-50, 164-71; Jones, *Papers on Psycho-Analysis,* pp. 664-88; Abra- ham, *Selected Papers on Psychoanalysis,* pp. 370-92.
[27] Empson, *Some Versions of Pastoral,* p. 60.

It is the same machinery, in the fearful case of Swift, that betrays not consciousness of the audience but a doubt of which he may himself have been unconscious. "Everything spiritual and valuable has a gross and revolting parody, very similar to it, with the same name. Only unremitting judgement can distinguish between them"; he set out to simplify the work of judgement by giving a complete set of obscene puns for it. The conscious aim was the defense of the Established Church against the reformers' Inner Light; only the psychoanalyst can wholly applaud the result. Mixed with his statement, part of what he satirized by pretending (too convincingly) to believe, the source of his horror, was "everything spiritual is really material; Hobbes and the scientists have proved this; all religion is really a perversion of sexuality."

The source of Swift's horror, according to Empson, is the discovery of that relation between higher and lower, spiritual and physical, which psychoanalysis calls sublimation. Swift hit upon the doctrine of sublimation as a new method for the psychological analysis of religion, specifically religious enthusiasm. His new method sees religious enthusiasm as the effect of what he calls the "Mechanical Operation of the Spirit." At the outset he distinguishes his psychology of religion from traditional naturalistic psychology, which treats religious enthusiasm as "the Product of Natural Causes, the effect of strong Imagination, Spleen, violent Anger, Fear, Grief, Pain, and the like." If you want a distinctive label for Swift's new psychology of religion, it can only be called psychoanalysis. The first step is to define religious enthusiasm as "a lifting up of the Soul or its Faculties above Matter." Swift then proceeds to the fundamental proposition that "the Corruption of the Senses is the Generation of the Spirit." By corruption of the senses Swift means repression, as is quite clear from his explanation:[28]

Because the Senses in Men are so many Avenues to the Fort of Reason, which in this Operation is wholly block'd up. All Endeavours must be therefore used, either to divert, bind up, stupify, fluster, and amuse the Senses, or else to justle them out of their Stations; and while they are either absent, or otherwise employ'd or engaged in a Civil War against each other, the Spirit enters and performs its Part.

[28] Swift, *Mechanical Operation of the Spirit*, pp. 174-76.

The doctrine that repression is the cause of sublimation is vividly implied in the analogy which Swift sets up for the "Mechanical Operation of the Spirit":[29]

> Among our Ancestors, the Scythians, there was a Nation, call'd Longheads, which at first began by a Custom among Midwives and Nurses, of molding, and squeezing, and bracing up the Heads of Infants; by which means, Nature shut out at one Passage, was forc'd to seek another, and finding room above, shot upwards, in the Form of a Sugar-Loaf.

Swift affirms not only that the spirit is generated by repression of bodily sensuousness, but also, as is implied by the analogy of the Scythian Longheads, that the basic structure of sublimation is, to use the psychoanalytical formula, displacement from below upward. Displacement from below upward, conferring on the upper region of the body a symbolic identity with the lower region of the body, is Swift's explanation for the Puritan cult of large ears: the ear is a symbolic penis. According to psychoanalysis, displacement of the genital function to another organ is the basic pattern in conversion hysteria. "Conversion hysteria genitalizes those parts of the body at which the symptoms are manifested"; maidenly blushing, for example, is a mild case of conversion hysteria—that is, a mild erection of the entire head.[30] According to Swift's analysis of the Puritans, "The Proportion of largeness, was not only lookt upon as an Ornament of the Outward Man, but as a Type of Grace in the Inward. Besides, it is held by Naturalists, that if there be a Protuberancy of Parts in the *Superiour* Region of the Body, as in the Ears and Nose, there must be a Parity also in the *Inferior.*" Hence, says Swift, the devouter Sisters "lookt upon all such extraordinary Dilations of that Member, as Protrusions of Zeal, or spiritual Excrescencies" and also "in hopes of conceiving a suitable Offspring by such a Prospect." [31] By this road Swift arrives at Freud's theorem on the identity of what is highest and lowest in human nature. In Freud's language: "Thus it is that what belongs to the lowest depths in the minds of each one of us is

[29] Swift, *Mechanical Operation of the Spirit*, p. 175.
[30] Ferenczi, *Further Contributions*, p. 90; Ferenczi, *Thalassa*, p. 14.
[31] Swift, *A Tale of a Tub*, p. 129.

changed, through this formation of the ideal, into what we value highest in the human soul." [32] In Swift's language:[33]

> Whereas the mind of Man, when he gives the Spur and Bridle to his Thoughts, doth never stop, but naturally sallies out into both extreams of High and Low, of Good and Evil; His first Flight of Fancy, commonly transports Him to Ideas of what is most Perfect, finished and exalted; till having soared out of his own Reach and Sight, not well perceiving how near the Frontiers of Height and Depth, border upon each other; With the same Course and Wing, he falls down plum into the lowest Bottom of Things; like one who travels the *East* into the *West;* or like a strait Line drawn by its own Length into a Circle.

Such is the demonic energy with which Swift pursues his vision that twice, once in *A Tale of a Tub* and once in *The Mechanical Operation of the Spirit,* he arrives at the notion of the unity of those opposites of all opposites, God and the Devil. Men, "pretending . . . to extend the Dominion of one Invisible Power, and contract that of the other, have discovered a gross Ignorance in the Natures of Good and Evil, and most horribly confounded the Frontiers of both. After Men have lifted up the Throne of their Divinity to the *Coelum Empyraeum;* . . . after they have sunk their *Principle* of *Evil* to the lowest Center . . . I laugh aloud, to see these Reasoners, at the same time, engaged in wise Dispute, about certain walks and Purlieus, whether they are in the Verge of God or the Devil, seriously debating, whether such and such Influences come into Men's Minds, from above or below, or whether certain Passions and Affections are guided by the Evil Spirit or the Good. . . . Thus do Men establish a Fellowship of Christ with Belial, and such is the Analogy they make between *cloven Tongues,* and *cloven Feet.*" [34] Empson has shown how and by what law of irony the partially disclaimed thought is Swift's own thought.

As we have argued elsewhere, psychoanalysis finds far-reaching resemblances between a sublimation and a neurotic symptom. Both

---

[32] *The Ego and the Id,* tr. J. Rivière (London, 1927), 48.
[33] Swift, *A Tale of a Tub,* p. 99.
[34] Swift, *Mechanical Operation of the Spirit,* pp. 179-80. Cf. Swift, *A Tale of a Tub,* pp. 99-100.

presuppose repression; both involve a displacement resulting from the repression of libido from the primary erogenous zones. Thus the psychoanalytic theory of sublimation leads on to the theory of the universal neurosis of mankind. In the words of Freud:[35]

> In one way the neuroses show a striking and far-reaching correspondence with the great social productions of art, religion and philosophy, while again they seem like distortions of them. We may say that hysteria is a caricature of an artistic creation, a compulsion neurosis, a caricature of a religion, and a paranoiac delusion, a caricature of a philosophic system.

Swift develops his doctrine of the universal neurosis of mankind in the "Digression concerning the Original, the Use and Improvement of Madness in a Commonwealth," in *A Tale of a Tub*. Here Swift attributes to Madness "the greatest Actions that have been performed in the World, under the Influence of Single Men; which are, *the Establishment of New Empires by Conquest: the Advance and Progress of New Schemes in Philosophy; and the contriving, as well as the propagating of New Religions*." Psychoanalysis must regret the omission of art, but applaud the addition of politics, to Freud's original list; Freud himself added politics in his later writings. And Swift deduces the universal neurosis of mankind from his notion of sublimation; in his words:

> For the *upper Region* of Man, is furnished like the *middle Region* of the Air; The Materials are formed from Causes of the widest Difference, yet produce at last the same Substance and Effect. Mists arise from the Earth, Steams from Dunghils, Exhalations from the Sea, and Smoak from Fire; yet all Clouds are the same in Composition, as well as Consequences: and the Fumes issuing from a Jakes, will furnish as comely and useful a Vapour, as Incense from an Altar. Thus far, I suppose, will easily be granted me; and then it will follow, that as the Face of Nature never produces Rain, but when it is overcast and disturbed, so Human Understanding, seated in the Brain, must be troubled and overspread by vapours, ascending from the lower Faculties, to water the Invention, and render it fruitful.

After a witty review of kings, philosophers, and religious fanatics Swift concludes: "If the *Moderns* mean by *Madness*, only a Dis-

[35] *The Basic Writings*, tr. and ed. A. A. Brill (New York, 1938): *Totem and Taboo*, 863-64.

turbance or Transposition of the Brain, by force of certain *Vapours* issuing up from the lower Faculties; then has this *Madness* been the Parent of all these mighty Revolutions, that have happened in *Empire,* in *Philosophy,* and in *Religion.*" And Swift ends the Digression on Madness with a humility and consistency psychoanalysis has never known, by applying his own doctrine to himself:[36]

> Even I myself, the Author of these momentous Truths, am a Person, whose Imaginations are hard-mouthed, and exceedingly disposed to run away with his *Reason,* which I have observed from long Experience to be a very light Rider, and easily shook off; upon which account, my Friends will never trust me alone, without a solemn Promise, to vent my Speculations in this, or the like manner, for the universal Benefit of Human kind.

Swift, as we have seen, sees in sublimation, or at least certain kinds of sublimation, a displacement upward of the genital function. So much was implied in his attribution of genital significance to the Puritans' large ears. He makes a similar, only more elaborately obscene, derivation of the nasal twang of Puritan preachers. He also speaks of "certain Sanguine Brethren of the first Class," that "in the Height and *Orgasmus* of their Spiritual exercise it has been frequent with them *****; immediately after which they found the *Spirit* to relax and flag of a sudden with the Nerves, and they were forced to hasten to a Conclusion." Swift explains all these phenomena with his notion of sublimation:[37]

> The Seed or Principle, which has ever put Men upon *Visions* in Things *Invisible,* is of a corporeal Nature. . . . The Spinal Marrow, being nothing else but a Continuation of the Brain, must needs create a very free Communication between the Superior Faculties and those below: And thus the *Thorn in the Flesh* serves for a *Spur* to the Spirit.

Not only the genital function but also the anal function is displaced upward, according to Swift. The general theorem is already stated in the comparison of the upper Region of Man to the middle Region of the Air, in which "the Fumes issuing from a Jakes, will

[36] Swift, *A Tale of a Tub,* pp. 102-103, 107-108, 114.
[37] Swift, *Mechanical Operation of the Spirit,* pp. 184-85, 188-89.

furnish as comely and useful a Vapour, as Incense from an Altar." [38]
The idea is developed in the image of religious enthusiasts as
Aeolists, or worshipers of wind. Swift is here punning on the word
"spirit," and as Empson says, "The language plays into his hands
here, because the spiritual words are all derived from physical
metaphors." [39] Psychoanalysis, of course, must regard language as
a repository of the psychic history of mankind, and the exploration
of words, by wit or poetry or scientific etymology, as one of the
avenues into the unconscious.[40] At any rate, Swift's wit, pursuing
his "Physicological Scheme" for satirical anatomy, "dissecting the
Carcass of Humane Nature," [41] asks where all this windy preaching comes from, and his answer gives all the emphasis of obscenity
to the anal factor:[42]

> At other times were to be seen several Hundreds link'd together
> in a circular Chain, with every Man a Pair of Bellows applied to his
> Neighbour's Breech, by which they blew up each other to the Shape
> and Size of a *Tun;* and for that Reason, with great Propriety of
> Speech, did usually call their Bodies, their *Vessels.* When by these and
> the like Performances, they were grown sufficiently replete, they
> would immediately depart, and disembogue for the Public Good, a
> plentiful Share of their Acquirements into their Disciples Chaps.

Another method of inspiration involves a Barrel instead of a
Bellows:

> Into this *Barrel,* upon Solemn Days, the Priest enters; where, hav-
> ing before duly prepared himself by the methods already described,
> a secret Funnel is also convey'd from his Posteriors, to the Bottom of
> the Barrel, which admits of new Supplies Inspiration from a *Northern*
> Chink or Crany. Whereupon, you behold him swell immediately to
> the Shape and Size of his *Vessel.* In this posture he disembogues whole
> Tempests upon his Auditory, as the Spirit from beneath gives him
> Utterance; which issuing *ex adytis,* and *penetralibus,* is not performed
> without much Pain and Gripings.

[38] Swift, *A Tale of a Tub*, p. 102.
[39] Empson, *op. cit.*, p. 60.
[40] *A General Introduction to Psycho-Analysis*, tr. J. Rivière (New York, 1953),
166, 174-5; and *Collected Papers*, IV, 184-91.
[41] Swift, *A Tale of a Tub*, pp. 37, 77.
[42] Swift, *A Tale of a Tub*, pp. 96, 98.

Nor is Swift's vision of sublimated anality limited to religious preaching or *A Tale of a Tub*. In *Strephon and Chloe* the malicious gossip of women is so explained:

> You'd think she utter'd from behind
> Or at her Mouth were breaking Wind.

And more generally, as Greenacre observes, there is throughout Swift "a kind of linking of the written or printed word with the excretory functions." [43] When Swift writes in a letter to Arbuthnot, "Let my anger break out at the end of my pen," [44] the psychoanalytically uninitiated may doubt the psychoanalytical interpretation. But Swift makes references to literary polemics (his own literary form) as dirt-throwing (compare the Yahoos). More generally he meditates that "mortal man is a broomstick," which "raiseth a mighty Dust where there was none before; sharing deeply all the while in the very same Pollutions he pretends to sweep away." [45] In the *Letter of Advice to a Young Poet,* he advocates the concentration of writers in a Grub Street, so that the whole town be saved from becoming a sewer: "When writers of all sizes, like freemen of cities, are at liberty to throw out their filth and excrementitious productions, in every street as they please, what can the consequence be, but that the town must be poisoned and become such another jakes, as by report of great travellers, Edinburgh is at night." [46] This train of thought is so characteristically Swift's that in the *Memoirs of Martinus Scriblerus,* now thought to have been written by Pope after talks with Arbuthnot and Swift, the story of Scriblerus' birth must be an inspiration of Swift's: "Nor was the birth of this great man unattended with prodigies: he himself has often told me, that on the night before he was born, Mrs. Scriblerus dreamed she was brought to bed of a huge ink-horn, out of which issued several large streams of ink, as it had been a fountain. This dream was by her husband thought to

---

[43] Greenacre, *op. cit.*, p. 56.
[44] Cf. Greenacre, *op. cit.*, p. 56.
[45] Swift, *A Tale of a Tub*, pp. 5, 63, 116; Swift, *A Meditation upon a Broomstick*, in *Prose Works of Jonathan Swift* (Oxford, 1939), I, 239-40.
[46] Swift, *Letter of Advice to a Young Poet*, in *Prose Works of Jonathan Swift* (London, 1907), XI, 108.

signify that the child should prove a very voluminous writer." [47]
Even the uninitiated will recognize the fantasy, discovered by psychoanalysis, of anal birth.

It would be wearisome to rehearse the parallels to Swift in psychoanalytical literature. The psychoanalysts, alas, think they can dispense with wit in the exploration of the unconscious. Fenichel in his encyclopedia of psychoanalytical orthodoxy refers to the "anal-erotic nature of speech" without intending to be funny.[48] Perhaps it will suffice to quote from Ferenczi's essay on the proverb "Silence is golden" for Ferenczi the proverb itself is one more piece of evidence on the anal character of speech:[49]

> That there are certain connections between anal erotism and speech I had already learnt from Professor Freud, who told me of a stammerer all whose singularities of speech were to be traced to anal phantasies. Jones too has repeatedly indicated in his writings the displacement of libido from anal activities to phonation. Finally I too, in an earlier article ("On Obscene Words") was able to indicate the connection between musical voice-culture and anal erotism.

Altogether Ernest Jones's essay on "Anal-Erotic Character Traits"[50] leaves us with the impression that there is no aspect of higher culture uncontaminated by connections with anality. And Swift leaves us with the same impression. Swift even anticipates the psychoanalytical theorem that an anal sublimation can be decomposed into simple anality. He tells the story of a furious conqueror who left off his conquering career when "the *Vapour* or *Spirit*, which animated the Hero's Brain, being in perpetual Circulation, seized upon that Region of the Human Body, so renown'd for furnishing the *ibeta Occidentalis*, and gathering there into a Tumor, left the rest of the World for that Time in Peace." [51]

The anal character of civilization is a topic which requires sociological and historical as well as psychological treatment. Swift turns to the sociology and history of anality in a poem called *A Panegyrick on the Dean*. The poem is written as if by Lady Acheson,

[47] Pope, *Works*, X, 281.
[48] Fenichel, *The Psychoanalytic Theory of Neurosis*, p. 312.
[49] Ferenczi, *Further Contributions*, p. 251.
[50] See above, note 26.
[51] Swift. *A Tale of a Tub*, p. 104.

the lady of the house at Market Hill where Swift stayed in 1729-
1730. In the form of ironic praise, it describes Swift's various roles
at Market Hill, as Dean, as conversationalist with the ladies, as
Butler fetching a bottle from the cellar, as Dairymaid churning
Butter. But the Dean's greatest achievement at Market Hills was
the construction of "Two Temples of magnifick Size," where—

> In sep'rate Cells the He's and She's
> Here pay their vows with *bended Knees,*

to the "gentle Goddess *Cloacine.*" As he built the two outhouses,
Swift seems to have meditated on the question of why we are
ashamed of and repress the anal function:

> Thee bounteous Goddess *Cloacine,*
> To Temples why do we confine?

The answer he proposes is that shame and repression of anality
did not exist in the age of innocence (here again we see how far
wrong Huxley's notion of Swift's "hatred of the bowels" is):

> When *Saturn* ruled the Skies alone
> That *golden* Age, to *Gold* unknown;
> This earthly Globe to thee assign'd
> Receiv'd the Gifts of all Mankind.

After the fall—the usurpation of Jove—came *"Gluttony* with
greasy Paws,*"* with her offspring "lolling *Sloth,"* "Pale *Dropsy,"*
"lordly *Gout,"* "wheezing *Asthma,"* "voluptuous *Ease,* the Child
of *Wealth"*—

> This bloated Harpy sprung from Hell
> Confin'd Thee Goddess to a Cell.

The corruption of the human body corrupted the anal function
and alienated the natural Cloacine:

> . . . unsav'ry Vaypours rose,
> Offensive to thy nicer Nose.

The correlative doctrine in psychoanalysis is of course the equation of money and feces. Swift is carried by the logic of the myth (myth, like wit, reaches into the unconscious) to make the same equation: the age of innocence, "the *golden* Age, to *Gold* unknown," had another kind of gold. The golden age still survives among the Swains of Northern Ireland—

> Whose Off'rings plac't in golden Ranks,
> Adorn our Christal River's Banks.

But the perspectives now opening up are too vast for Swift, or for us:

> But, stop ambitious Muse, in time;
> Nor dwell on Subjects too sublime.

What Gulliver Knew

by Joseph Horrell

1

Travels into Several Remote Nations of the World is neat and symmetrical in form, its four parts of about the same length, the first two with eight chapters each, the last two with eleven, plus an extra chapter as a conclusion. The "putative devices" are props to realism: an Introduction by the editor, "Richard Sympson," addressed to the reader; a portrait of the author and traveler, "Captain Lemuel Gulliver, of Redriff Ætat. suae 58," who was, as we learn from the title page, "first a Surgeon, and then a Captain of several Ships"; maps (with spouting whales) locating Lilliput, Brobdingnag, Laputa, and Houyhnhnms' Land in relation to known lands, with dates of discovery and other documentation; and (in the Faulkner edition of 1735) an Advertisement and a Letter from Captain Gulliver to his "Cousin" Sympson complaining of errors in early editions which might reflect upon the author's veracity. The dull gravity of all this environmental detail, along with the realistic framework of each part as factual in style as a ship's log, certifies the authenticity which readers expect in works of autobiography, history, or travel. Prose is normally the vehicle of truth, and what is Swift's fiction must be Captain Gulliver's "faithful History" of his travels. Thus Swift insinuates his classic of satire into the precincts of fiction. One historian of the English novel says that *Gulliver's Travels* "stands beside *Robinson Crusoe* as a

"What Gulliver Knew," by Joseph Horrell. Originally published in *The Sewanee Review*, LI, No. 4 (Autumn 1943), 476-504. Reprinted here in revised form by permission of the author and *The Sewanee Review*.

classic of realism. . . . Defoe might well have been responsible for all the preliminaries ushering Mr. Gulliver upon the scene."

Engineering all this machinery and keeping it operating amounts to little more than mastery of formalistic detail. But Swift possessed substantial (if little-used) talents in fiction such as a professional fiction writer might envy. We could make an impressive catalogue of examples: his extraordinary (for his day) skill at dialogue, drawn through an ear attuned to the cadence and idiom of actual speech, perhaps a by-product of his absorbing interest in the art of conversation; his sensitivity to locale and scene, enabling him to reproduce persons and place in the round (the Viceroy's household, Stella at Wood Park, holiday discomforts at Quilca, the domestic economy of Market Hill), or the not so round (the Irish Senate, the Court, the Royal family, Walpole); his "characters" of more abstract origin, all depressingly real (threadbare poets, starving pedants, poxed queans, rapacious politicians); his "undeviating attention to the point at issue" in telling a story (a quality Scott admired). Reading the world rather than books, he found "Isaac Bickerstaff" on a locksmith's sign in Longacre, which gave Addison and Steele the occasion (as Prior said) "of living seven years upon one of your thoughts." Swift's surroundings were registered on his senses wherever he found himself: his Bury Street lodgings in St. James's, the smoky inn at Holyhead where he waited for the packet boat, miserable Irish cabins. These talents might be considered superfluous in a person whose consuming ambition was to be a bishop. As a writer Swift was a "natural."

Take Defoe's fictional talents one by one, and you will find that Swift possesses most of them in equal or greater measure, but without their center. What Swift lacks is Defoe's coherence of purpose. Swift can do this or that, but he rarely musters all his resources because fiction is only a means to an end. His world has declined so catastrophically from its "original" that it cannot generate innocent narratives worth pursuing for their own sake. Defoe's always pressing obligation to moralize is smothered in the sheer delight he takes in his material; but Swift's moral judgments are so overpowering as to be regenerative, distorting his material, so to speak, by their paralytic effect on certain areas of sensibility. One of his favorite poets was Lucretius, but in the metaphorical representation of the great theme of corruption and generation he could not

hear, as Lucretius did, the cry of a new-born babe above the
funeral wail. Moll Flanders and Robinson Crusoe, ordinary people
from the mainstream of life, not literary casts from heroic molds,
reel under the blows of fortune, but triumph over every adversity
of society and nature. Defoe gives us a new kind of hero based on
a conviction about man. Gulliver develops an appetite for experience which is almost heroic, but he is only Swift's refractive window
on the world. He marks an ultimate in the "progress" from the
Odyssean hero, experience of the world reducing him to a man
always at a loss, a man who rejects human society for that of the
horse. Swift's object, it is true, lies beyond fiction, but the fictional
aspects of *Gulliver's Travels* are possibly more important to us
than they would be if the work was a simon-pure fiction, because
it is of the essence of Swift's scheme that the point of contact for
our sensuous perception of his satire is an outlandish story. Not
only that, the story is the datum for the dual perception which his
irony requires.

II

When we look at Swift's style narrowly, we find it almost true
that "the rogue never hazards a metaphor," and Gulliver obedi-
ently tells us that in his "faithful History" he has not been "so
studious of Ornament as of Truth." But in a broader sense metaphor is with Swift a "mode of apprehension" (to use Middleton
Murry's phrase). The fiction itself symbolizes the pettiness, grossness, rational absurdity, and animality which make man's pride an
absurd vice. For those ideas which can be conveyed by relative
physical magnitudes, as in the first two books, the symbolism is a
rather simple matter of magnification and minification. Providing
material for sensuous perception in the third and fourth books is
a more difficult undertaking. Here Swift must exercise his "mar-
vellous powers of making abstract thought luminous" (Craik). This
is where he comes into comparison with Dante, whose physical
embodiments of sin are repugnant to our senses.

The success of Swift's fiction, and hence of his satire, largely
depends on a persuasive accumulation of circumstantial and ironic

detail, and (what is more important) on certain manipulations of detail. The following are rough and ready stylistic paradigms:

> He is taller by almost the Breadth of my Nail, than any of his Court; which alone is enough to strike an Awe into the Beholders [*the Emperor in Lilliput*].

> She was very good natured, and not above forty Foot high, being little for her Age [*his nursemaid Glumdalclitch in Brobdingnag*].

> I afterwards saw five or six of different Ages, the youngest not above two Hundred Years old, who were brought to me at several Times by some of my Friends [*the Struldbrugs*].

> I took a second Leave of my Master: But as I was going to prostrate myself to kiss his Hoof, he did me the Honour to raise it gently to my Mouth [*the Houyhnhnm Master*].

To provide for our dual perception, which his irony requires, Swift loads innocent detail, so that our acceptance of a normal version of experience involves our entertaining another which is abnormal, but which is really the meat in the sandwich. In word, phrase, and larger unit Swift employs a subordinative technique of weaving the "odd, grotesque, and wild" (the qualities he assigned to humor) into the texture of dully plausible statement of fact. In *Gulliver's Travels* there is a constant shuttling back and forth between real and unreal, normal and absurd, especially in the early chapters of each book, until our standards of credulity are so relaxed that we are ready to buy a pig in a poke. Swift's fiction conditions us for imposture, and his readers are in more than one sense his victims.

As for the accommodative process in the first two books, there is some truth in Dr. Johnson's dictum, "When once you have thought of big men and little men, it is very easy to do all the rest." The "rest," in other words, is careful execution of the scheme. The more difficult problem of style arises in the third and fourth books because the differences between normal and abnormal cannot be symbolized quantitatively. These books are about qualities of mind, or rationality, and the scale is intellectual. (Here Swift loses many of his readers—all the children and a disappointing number of adults.) The emphatic real and muted unreal are still with us, but no longer with our perception fixed upon size. The

aputian episode is about hyperintellectuals (they have departed
the world as the soul leaves the body), who distastefully perform
the minimal functions of physical life on their island floating in
the air, while they devote their energies to spinning gossamer-thin
speculations or (what is worse) to projects based on speculations,
like extracting sunbeams from cucumbers or softening marble for
pincushions. More difficult than making man appear miniscule or
gigantic, Swift must embody qualities of mind in symbolic shapes.
Gulliver had never seen until now "a Race of Mortals so singular
in their Shapes, Habits, and Countenances."

In the Laputian world of highfalutin nonsense the Flapper is
the most effective symbol.[1] The ruling class of the Flying Island,
rapt in a vortex of speculation, enjoy the separation of the intellect
from the senses. They appear with their heads reclined to right
or left, with one eye turned inward, the other upward to the
zenith. The Flappers, a serving class, stimulate the senses of their
bemused lords by touching the eye or ear with bladders containing little pebbles or dried peas. (The milkmaid saved Thales
from falling into the well.) The symbolism is extended to favorite
Laputian subjects, music and mathematics, with cycloidal puddings
and ducks trussed up into the shape of fiddles, so that even at
table the Laputians are not far removed from their intense wool-
gathering. In this book we have not only the usual sprinkling of
jaw-breaking foreign names, but also the jargon of science (calcine,
diurnal, aqueous, percolate, seminal), which supplants to some
extent the commonplace words to which magnitudes can be
assigned.

III

The unity of *Gulliver's Travels* is re-enforced by themes which
are developed in the framework of the voyages and in the voyages
themselves. Those in the framework Swift uses with his customary

[1] The symbolism of Laputa is reminiscent of the Aeolists, who occasion Swift's
marathon etymological pun in the *Tale of a Tub*; but without the "metaphysical
conjectures" which distinguish Swift's "unconfined humor" of the earlier period.
The tensile fable of the *Tale* cannot be stretched to cover all that Swift wants
to say (hence the digressions), but in *Gulliver's Travels* he submits to the limitations imposed by his fiction.

frugality both as devices of realism and as motivation for Gulliver
rejection of man: his diminishing affection for his "domestic
Pledges," until they become hateful as Yahoos; his mistreatment a
the hands of his comrades; the growing malevolence of fortun
the frustration of his "insatiable Desire" of seeing foreign coun
tries. Swift also finds symbolic value in fictional details of th
framework. Gulliver's first voyage comes to grief when his ship
splits on a rock (*chance*). In the second, while they are ashore
searching for water, his shipmates, pursued by a Brobdingnagian
desert him (*cowardice*). During the third voyage pirates overhaul
his ship, and a fellow-Christian, failing to have him cast overboard
talks the more charitable Japanese captain into setting him adrift
in a canoe (*malevolence*). On the fourth voyage the mutinous crew
turn to piracy and exile Gulliver, their captain, on a deserte
shore (*treachery*). Acts of man are apparently more to be feared
than acts of God.

The four books themselves are linked by contrasts, and each
illuminates its predecessors. The nature of the symbolism makes
this obvious for the first two books, but it is easy to overlook the
links between the second and third and the third and fourth
Swift intends to offset the useful mathematics of the Brobding
nagians with the impractical mathematical interests of the Lapu
tians, who measure Gulliver for a suit of clothes by taking his alti
tude by a quadrant (the clothes don't fit). In the third book he i
preoccupied with immortality, or the separation of body and soul
The indifference of the Houyhnhnms to approaching death, o
time, is a commentary on the morbid picture of the Struldbrugs
whose immortality is a living death.

The continuous themes of the first three books are necessary
motivation for the last, where Gulliver thinks he has found a
vantage (i.e., that of the horse) for evaluating his experience o
man. In praising Lilliputian law he wished to be understood to
mean the "original Institutions" and "not the most scandalous
Corruptions in which these People are fallen by the degenerate
Nature of Man." In Brobdingnag he read treatises of morals and
history which showed "how diminutive, contemptible, and helpless
an Animal was Man in his own Nature," excelled by "one Creature
in Strength, by another in Speed, by a third in Foresight, by a
fourth in Industry," and that "Nature was degenerated in these
latter declining Ages of the World." At Glubdubdrib, "As every

erson called up made exactly the same Appearance he had done
n the World, it gave me melancholy Reflections to observe how
nuch the Race of human Kind was degenerate among us, within
hese Hundred Years past." Before he was disillusioned with it,
he immortality of the Struldbrugs promised to allow him to see
the several Gradations by which Corruption steals into the World,
nd oppose it in every Step," so that he might "prevent that con-
inual Degeneracy of human Nature, so justly complained of in
ll Ages." The "general Tradition" concerning the Yahoos holds
hat those in the Country of Horses derive from a pair from over
he sea, who, being deserted by their companions, "and degenerat-
ng by Degrees, became in Process of Time, much more savage
han those of their own Species in the Country from whence these
wo Originals came." Following Gulliver's account of his own
countrymen, the Houyhnhnm Master "looked upon us as a Sort
of Animals to whose Share, by what Accident he could not con-
ecture, some small Pittance of *Reason* had fallen, whereof we made
no other Use than by its Assistance to aggravate our *natural* Corruptions, and to acquire new ones which Nature had not given us."

There is so much incidental satire in the first three books that
we may form the habit of bypassing the fiction to get at it. In the
fourth book this short cut leads to a dead end. The symbols by
which Swift assimilates all his satire are so deeply embedded in the
fiction that ignoring his indirect method only leads to dismissal
of this book as disjointed, illogical, or beside the point: to vexation
without diversion. Swift symbolizes in the Yahoo the intellectual
themes which he has woven into the fiction: that man, as animal,
is less comely and less well adapted to his natural environment
than most others of the animal kingdom; that reason in civilized
man produces evil more often than good, accentuating natural
vices and making man more dangerous than brutes; that the
natural tendency of man to degenerate as the world ages can be—
but most likely will not be—countered by the assertion of his unique
rational powers, which are themselves vestigial or corrupted.[2] Much
of what we have previously been told about man's capacity for
evil we can now see, hear, smell, and feel in the Yahoo.

[2] The Pyrrhonism in Swift's view of nature and man can be found in Montaigne's *Apology for Raymond Sebond.* The study of the "sources" of *Gulliver's
Travels* is relatively profitless in understanding the book because Swift acquired
his intellectual background elsewhere.

The fiction is also the means by which Swift focuses the scattere
rays of his satire, shifting from foreign to domestic scenes, fror
institutions to individuals, from mankind to man, from others t
ourselves. The fourth book closes in on the subject. Among petty
gross, or absurd people, Gulliver can take comfort in his own kinc
and foreign criticism of one's own country can be attributed t
the effects of a "confined Education." We enjoy for a time a simila
detachment. During Gulliver's voyages, as we view successive as
pects of man, we concede similarities of customs, habits, and instr
tutions, but without any personal involvement. We can even ex
clude ourselves, as Gulliver does himself, from "the Bulk of you
Natives" whom the Brobdingnagian King concludes to be a "mos
pernicious Race of little odious Vermin." As Swift said in an earlie
work, "Satyr is a sort of *Glass,* wherein Beholders do generally dis
cover every body's Face but their Own." But the fourth book doe
away with all that. The fiction forces upon Gulliver the "recog
nition" that all are Yahoos of the race of men, and his mock-tragi
"catastrophe" is exile from his adopted Houyhnhnmland. Wher
the Houyhnhnm Master examines Gulliver's body and pronounce
him Yahoo, this merciless scrutiny, by Swift's contrivance, fall
equally upon ourselves. A good many readers, like Gulliver, neve
recover, because they do not submit to the fiction by which Swift
with his finest irony, establishes a vantage outside man: that o
the horse.

IV

The fourth book introduces this thematic complication. Natural
uncivilized man is the theme of this book, just as man is the sub
ject of the entire work, but the thematic Yahoo is counterpointed
by the Houyhnhnm, so that we see Gulliver for the first time among
creatures like and unlike his species. This permits the sequence of
recognition, crisis, catastrophe, and denouement, plus a remark
able curtain speech by Gulliver. Previously, Gulliver has felt no
real conflict with the natives discovered in his voyages, because
the physical and intellectual plane in which he exists is supposedly
above, or below, or unlike that of the creatures around him,
though he occasionally betrays a missionary-like zeal (this soon
starts backfiring) to educate the inhabitants in the superior man-

ners and institutions of his own country. But this patronizing attitude toward "foreigners" weakens under the impact of experience
until, during the fourth adventure, Gulliver concludes that they,
he, and the Yahoos are essentially the same.

The introduction of the horse was Swift's most brilliant and
humorous inspiration in *Gulliver's Travels*. No doubt he had in
mind the rationale of the fable, "a narrative in which beings irrational, and sometimes inanimate, *arbores loquuntur, non tantum
ferae,* are, for the purpose of moral instruction, feigned to act
and speak with human interests and passions" (Dr. Johnson). But
his fiction requires that he establish this rationale only gradually,
and by the time he has done so those who ignore the fiction, or
read it literally as children do the first two books, are condemning
this "outrage on humanity," not just because of its satire, though
this is "utterly inhuman" and "intellectually inferior," but on the
technical ground that it "has not even the merit of being consistent": so Hugh Walker in *English Satire and Satirists*. Thackeray
finds great literary proficiency in the last book, but deplores its
message. What is the message? Professor Willey in *The Eighteenth
Century Background* surely misreads it when he speaks of Swift's
distinction "between rational man (Houyhnhnm) and irrational
man (Yahoo)." Anyone who seriously believes that Swift, as distinguished from Gulliver, wishes to offer the Houyhnhnm as *animal
rationale,* or an ideal for man, must somehow take seriously Swift's
picture of Gulliver, at home, gravely conversing with his horses. It
is no shame, says Gulliver, "to learn wisdom from Brutes"; and one
can do so, as the rationale of the fable indicates, without identifying
the animal who speaks oracularly of reason with rationality itself.
(Gulliver tried to become a member of the Houyhnhnm family, but
this absurdity led to his "catastrophe," which was "Exile" to his
own species at home.) Let's see how this rationale is introduced.

The attention that Swift devotes to the fictional preliminaries of
each part is essential in bridging our passage from the real to the
fantastic, and the same process takes place in the fourth book, only
the accommodative process is more subtle, the fantastic world more
incredible. To the extent that Swift is successful we accept in Gulliver's mind, though not unreservedly in our own, the transposition
of two links in the chain of being, and if we catch the mood of
Swift's ironic humor we may even enjoy the absurdities that ensue.
We must follow this process more carefully than is generally done

Ashore, after finding "great plenty of Grass, and several Fields of Oats," Gulliver falls into a beaten road "where I saw many Tracks of human Feet, and some of Cows, but most of Horses." He then suffers his first disgusting encounter with the Yahoos, who are de-cribed in detail, with incidental comparisons of these "Beasts" with goats and squirrels (just as, in Lilliput and Brobdingnag, man is compared with diminutive and contemptible creatures like weasels), but with no recognition that they fit the tracks of human feet, which are left for the time being unaccounted for.

Next, Gulliver meets the animal whose arrival drives the Yahoos away, and there is no doubt as to its species. It is a horse, a gentle creature which looks at him "with a very mild Aspect, never offering the least Violence." When another arrives the two horses neigh to each other "as if" conversing and they "seem" to deliberate. (These qualifying words soon disappear as the horse becomes Houyhnhnm.) "I was amazed to see such Actions and Behaviour in brute Beasts; and concluded with myself, that if the Inhabitants of this Country were endued with a proportionable Degree of Reason, they must needs be the wisest People upon Earth." This thought gives him so much comfort that he hastens on following the horses with the hope of meeting "with any of the Natives."

Thus very quickly Swift has established the terms and concepts of his fiction. The cows are not brought upon the scene until later, for a reason which is apparent in Swift's handling of detail: the horses fit the horse tracks; the "Inhabitants," those supremely wise people as yet unseen, fit the many tracks of human feet; the Yahoos are cattle: so Gulliver thinks. In his nasty encounter with the Yahoos he was careful to strike one with the flat side of his sword, "fearing the Inhabitants might be provoked against me, if they should come to know, that I had killed or maimed any of their Cattle." Swift has been careful to make Gulliver's detailed description of the Yahoos omit that their feet, observed several times, are human, though the "shape" of these animals "a little discomposed me."

Swift goes over the same terms and concepts again. Gulliver fol-lows the horse several miles to the buildings, furnished like stables, with nags and mares sitting on their hams and busy at domestic tasks, where he gets his presents ready for the "Master and Mistress of the House," anxiously waiting, while the horse neighs, "to hear some answers in a human Voice." This well-trained horse must belong to "some Person of great Note," but that a "Man of Quality" should be served by horses is beyond Gulliver's comprehension. There is still no human voice, and Gulliver looks around only to find more racks and mangers. He begins to see his situation for what it is. "I rubbed my Eyes often, but the same Objects still occurred." And so Gulliver enters a world in which the horse is supreme: the inhabitant, the native, and the master.

V

If Gulliver had found those "Inhabitants" with a degree of reason "proportionable" to that of the horses, Swift might have produced a Utopia which could furnish material for Pope's *Essay on Man*. This was impossible for him to do. Educated in the older century, preferring to study mankind in history rather than philosophy, in experience rather than speculation, in practice rather than theory, he took a traditional and conservative view of the possibilities of man. In his mind the Ancients tower over the Moderns, not just in the commonwealth of wit and learning, which is the field of the *Tale of a Tub* and the *Battle of the Books,* but also in political and social institutions, as we see when the necromancers of Glubbdub-drib produce a Roman Senate for comparison with its modern counterpart. Swift found it more within the realm of possibility and human experience to imagine an ideal horse than an ideal man, but rational man remained nonetheless an ideal, and those "wisest People upon Earth," whose existence Gulliver assumes, are the "fourth proportional" that we solve for from three given terms:

Horse : Houyhnhnm : : Yahoo : (Rational Man)

Or we can substitute for the human terms those of Swift's well-known letter to Pope, in which (opposing the optimistic views of Pope and Bolingbroke) he asserts the falsity of *animal rationale* as a definition of man, and the aptness of *rationis capax:*

Horse : Houyhnhnm :: *Animal rationis capax* : *Animal rationale*

The Utopia that Swift did not write would have presented the extreme terms, ordinary horses and rational men; whereas the fourth book, with some exaggeration of the mean terms to sharpen the satiric contrast, is a matter of "the many Virtues of those excellent *Quadrupeds* placed in opposite View to human Corruptions."

Very soon these remarkable animals, first described as "brute Beasts," come to be known to Gulliver as "Houyhnhnms" after the noises they make, though he later tells us the word "in their Tongue, signifies a *Horse;* and in its Etymology, *the Perfection of Nature.*" The superior qualities of the Houyhnhnms are of two kinds: first, their physical characteristics of strength, comeliness, and speed, which are natural attributes of the horse, precisely as Gulliver describes this noblest animal of his own country; and secondly, their virtues of friendship, benevolence, rationality, and devotion to duty, all of which are privative. The logic in Gulliver's attribution to the horse of these virtues lies in their negation of the corresponding vices in the Yahoos. Horses do not shirk, do not lie, do no evil; and so the Houyhnhnms are industrious, truthful, and virtuous. Vice is a negation of reason and nature of which the Houyhnhnm is incapable, living as this species does in paradisial ignorance of human treachery, lying, and cruelty, with "no Word in their Language to express any thing that is *evil,* except what they borrow from the Deformities or Ill Qualities of the *Yahoos.*" This attribution is a gradual process: "At first, indeed, I did not feel that natural Awe which the *Yahoos* and all other Animals bear towards them; but it grew upon me by Degrees, much sooner than I imagined." Swift has the situation turned upside down by the beginning of the third chapter when the Houyhnhnm Master, his children, and servants, as they teach Gulliver their language, which is pronounced through the nose and throat, look upon it "as a Prodigy, that a brute Animal should discover such Marks of a rational Creature."

This acknowledgment of the superior qualities of the horse, a somewhat gradual process of abstraction, proceeds inversely with Gulliver's recognition that men and Yahoos are the same species. Very early the "master Horse" (not yet a "Houyhnhnm") compares Yahoos with him. "My Horror and Astonishment are not to be described, when I observed, in this abominable Animal, a perfect human Figure. . . . The Fore-feet of the *Yahoo* differed from my Hands in nothing else, but the Length of the Nails, the Coarseness and Brownness of the Palms, and the Hairiness on the Backs." But the horses, ignorant of the deceitfulness of art, cannot at first regard Gulliver's clothes as other than a natural difference between him and the Yahoo. Gulliver conceals "the Secret of my Dress, in order to distinguish myself as much as possible, from that cursed Race of *Yahoos*," until the Sorrel Nag, the Houyhnhnm Master's valet, discovers him asleep undressed. In the "unmasking" scene which follows, the Houyhnhnm Master concludes from an examination of Gulliver's body that "I must be a perfect *Yahoo*." This encounter between civilized man and natural horse is described within the general terms of Swift's favorite "clothes philosophy": clothes are, Gulliver says, "prepared by Art" for the sake of decency and to protect man from the inclemency of weather, covering also "those Parts that Nature taught us to conceal"; but the Houyhnhnm Master, who does not need the protection and feels no shame, cannot understand "why Nature should teach us to conceal what Nature had given." This little allegory of Art and Nature plays upon the story as it unfolds in the rest of the book: whether civilized man, who is physically inferior to the horse, or indeed, as the Houyhnhnm Master points out, to the Yahoo, will use the art which his rationality affords him to perfect himself, harmonizing Art with Nature, or will use this art, by accentuating the propensity to vice of a fallen creature, to add to the rich vocabulary of civilized "Enormities" almost inexplicable to the innocent Houyhnhnms.

With superficial resemblance established, Swift drives home our essential identification with the Yahoo. In Chapters V and VI, Gulliver reports to the Houyhnhnm Master on man in "civilized" society, and in Chapter VII the Houyhnhnm Master, who has listened with care, draws devastating parallels between the highly developed vices of the European Yahoos and those propensities to vice in the physically superior Yahoos of Houyhnhnmland, observing "what Parity there was in our Natures." Gulliver has reported that in a civilized "Man of Quality, . . . The imperfections of his Mind run parallel with those of his Body; being a Composition of Spleen, Dulness, Ignorance, Caprice, Sensuality and Pride." From Gulliver's larger recital of the "Enormities" of civilized Yahoos endowed, like himself, with reason, the Houyhnhnm Master "dreaded lest the Corruption of that Faculty might be worse than Brutality itself." This is (in Dr. Johnson's phrase) the "moral instruction" that Swift offers in his fabulous tale. Is it groundless in human experience to fear that Art and Reason will corrupt, if they do not refine, man's nature? Does not the smell of burning human flesh which hangs like a nauseous miasma over this century remind us of enormities more revolting than Swift, with all his misanthropy, could imagine?

Has Swift's transposition of man and horse, intended to affront our pride of species, made his "warning" to mankind a "philosophic pill" that is unswallowable? The positive contribution of nineteenth century criticism is the horrified emphasis it lays on this shocking and degrading incongruity, but this criticism is misapplied if we insist upon seeing the incongruity only in one sense and only from the point of view of the offended party, man. With his ironic humor Swift compels us to see man's behavior, inside and outside civilized society, from the detached viewpoint of a horse, and the fourth book rings with horse laughs. With subtle modulations of "foot" and "hoof" Swift induces us to accept Gulliver's picture of a white mare threading a needle. If there is a case to be made for the viciousness of man, Swift has made it in the fourth book with a savage indignation tempered by humor.[3]

VI

Now, let us return once more to Swift's subordinative technique, this time with reference to his humor, which is implicit in it. A more precise description of the method as applied in the fourth book is found in what Ogden and Richards call the "utraquistic subterfuge," or the unfair use in argument of diverse referents for a single term. (In fiction, of course, the notion of fairness does not apply, because we should not be reading it if we are not willing to be deceived.) As we have suggested before, Swift is a master of subterfuge, who can be "utraquistic" on a systematic scale: witness his use of "Brute" always for Yahoo, sometimes for Gulliver, occasionally for Houyhnhnm, depending on which leg of his irony he wishes to carry his weight at a given moment; or "Quadruped" for Houyhnhnm and Yahoo; or "Cattle" for cows and Yahoos. Indeed, Swift turns the method upside down, using pairs of terms drawn from different animal species for the same referent: "House" for the Houyhnhnm lodging, "Stable" for the Yahoo; or "forefeet" and

---

[3] Perhaps the only author who has approached the denunciative power of Swift, with a similar blend of irony and humor, is Mark Twain, whose account of Huck's guilty conscience at attempting to free a runaway slave, Nigger Jim, is a scathing indictment of society and its corruption of man (*Huckleberry Finn*, chap. xxxi). But when their raft is adrift on the great river, without intrusions from civilized society on the bank, Huck and Jim live a timeless idyll such as Swift would not allow to natural man.

"hands" in referring to Gulliver, with subtle shifts between human and animal emphasis. Just as Gulliver observes that "Friendship" and "Benevolence" are the primary virtues of the Houyhnhnms, so he finds these qualities in his domestic animals at home: "they live in great Amity with me, and Friendship to each Other." Likewise in learning the Houyhnhnm language: after five months Gulliver is able to express himself "tolerably well"; and of his stable companions at home (horses in his own country, he had told the Houyhnhnm Master, have not the "least Tincture" of reason), "My Horses understand me tolerably well; I converse with them at least four Hours every Day." Thus Swift manages whatever degree of absurdity he wishes to convey: we have pictures of Houyhnhnms sitting on their haunches eating dinner, or riding in sledges drawn by Yahoos, or neighing their observations on Gulliver's "bad Accent" or his affectation of walking on his "hinder Feet." Nearly always, after probing here and there, Swift drives the point home in one blow, as in Gulliver's leave-taking of the Houyhnhnm Master: "I took a second Leave of my Master: But as I was going to prostrate myself to kiss his Hoof, he did me the Honour to raise it gently to my Mouth." Of all Swift's critics only Thackeray, who regarded this as the best stroke of humor in this "dreadful allegory," has brought together the three essential notions (logic, absurdity, humor): "It is truth topsy-turvy, entirely logical and absurd."

A "utraquism" which overlies *Gulliver's Travels* like a blanket is the theme of truth. The protestations of truth which Gulliver makes through three adventures are carried into the fourth, but there, with all the evils of Yahooism exposed, the concept of lying appears. For this, as for any other human evil, the Houyhnhnms have no word, and the Master can understand lying only as "saying the Thing which is not" (a definition which serves as well for irony). Not only does the theme of truth *versus* mendacity pervade Gulliver's narrative, but Swift surrounds the book with like considerations. "Richard Sympson," the supposed editor, tells us the author was renowned for veracity among his neighbors at Redriff, where it was proverbial that a thing "was as true as if Mr. Gulliver had spoke it." The early editions carried under Captain Gulliver's portrait some lines from Persius commending honesty (replaced in the Faulkner edition with *"Splendide Mendax"* from Horace). When the book first appeared, Swift wrote Pope, "A Bishop here said that book was full of improbable lies, and for his part, he hardly believed a word of it." Of all Swift's acquaintances Dr. Arbuthnot ("Who dares to Irony pretend") was peculiarly qualified to comment in the spirit of the occasion, because he had adumbrated the basic principles of "phantateustics" in the *Art of Political Lying* ("Tis very pretty," Swift wrote Stella, "but not so obvious to be understood"). A lie, by Arbuthnot's principle, is better contradicted by another lie than by the truth: if it is reported that the Pretender was at London, one would not contradict this by saying he was never in England, but would prove by eye-witnesses that he came no farther than Greenwich, and then went back again; or if it is spread about that a great person is dying of some disease, one would not declare the truth that the person is in good health and never had the disease, but would report that he is slowly recovering from it. In this spirit Arbuthnot wrote Swift that a friend of his had fallen in company with the master of a ship, who told him that he was very well acquainted with Gulliver, but that the printer was mistaken, he lived in Wapping and not in Rotherhithe.

The "utraquistic" nature of Gulliver's protestations of truth is part and parcel of Swift's "hum'rous, biting Way" (a "bite" being a verbal prank which imposes upon the credulity of its victim). He surrounds the book with the same protestations as those inside it, just as his writings coalesce with ambient life because he drew no sharp line between the spheres of action and thought. In the last chapter we see how much secret joy he took in his "bite" on the reader, on us. Gulliver allows that he has not claimed for the Crown the countries he has discovered, but wishes that all travelers might be required to take an oath before the Lord Chancellor as to their truthfulness, for he is indignant "to see the credulity of mankind so impudently abused." With the example of the illustrious Houyhnhnms before him, he has made it a maxim to "adhere strictly to the truth"; whereupon he quotes from the *Aeneid* a similar protestation by Sinon, who has just told the Trojans a lie about a horse.

The Final Comedy of
Lemuel Gulliver

by John F. Ross

Nominally, everyone regards *Gulliver's Travels* as one of the world's very great satires; the difficult intellectual feat, apparently, is to realize how satiric it is. Critical appraisals of *Gulliver,* at any rate, fall into confusion over the fourth voyage. Confronted by Swift's most unrelenting and severe attack on the Yahoo nature of man, the critic, from some obscure fellow feeling, refuses to read *Gulliver* to the end as complex satire. He thereby misses the final comic absurdity inherent in what is the climax not only of the fourth voyage, but of the satire as a whole. Swift may not be a comic figure, but Gulliver decidedly is.

I

Consider, in this regard, the common evaluation of Gulliver as voiced by Thackeray, Leslie Stephen, and their twentieth century followers. Whatever their differences, and they have many, they are in substantial agreement on several points. (1) *Gulliver* is one of the world's great satires, and perhaps the most severe. (2) Voyage IV is its climax. And this voyage is plainspoken, terrible, and overwhelming, upsetting in the extreme to our normally optimistic view of man's nature and achievement. (3) The Yahoos are not a true repre-

"The Final Comedy of Lemuel Gulliver," by John F. Ross. From *Studies in the Comic,* University of California Publications in English, VIII, No. 2 (1941), 175-196. Reprinted by permission of the author and the University of California Press.

sentation of mankind, nor can horses talk and reason. (4) It follows from (2) and (3) that the fourth voyage is indecent and shameful, an insult to humanity. (5) Since Swift lost his mind at an advanced age, he was insane when, years before, he wrote the fourth voyage. (6) Therefore (the conclusion is expressed or implicit) it is advisable not to read this particular work of art to its conclusion, but to stop halfway—that is to say, with the end of the second voyage.

A more logical conclusion for those who hold this attitude is this: great and severe satire should never be written, and if written, should be publicly burned—and the satirist with it. But logic has little enough to do with the matter; the attitude is self-contradictory. It resolves itself really into an acknowledgment of Swift's greatness and an admission of the validity of his satiric attack even in the fourth voyage, coupled with a determined refusal to admit that his attack is valid. The rationalization of the situation is not convincing, even when Swift's insanity is thrown in for good measure.

More thoughtful modern critics have abandoned this attitude, yet they too are troubled by Voyage IV. Severe satire, insults to humanity, and madness appear to worry them little; they have other objections. Something has gone wrong with Swift's craftsmanship. The last voyage is psychologically unconvincing. Even if we accept the Yahoos, we cannot accept the Houyhnhnms; and furthermore, the drab and limited life of the horses is wholly unsatisfactory as a Utopia, as Swift himself should have known. Perhaps it is simply that, carried away by the impetus of his severe attack, Swift has lost control. Of the fourth voyage, W. A. Eddy says in his critical study of *Gulliver*, "someone has blundered, and I fear me it is Swift." Ricardo Quintana, in his careful and penetrating study of Swift, has many doubts concerning the last voyage, and shakes his head over its "sensationalism." This modern type of analysis is on much firmer ground than the older attitude, and is not to be carelessly dismissed. Yet in it an old error persists: by identifying the later Gulliver too completely with Swift, it takes the fourth voyage much too literally as a statement of Swift's final position. For instance, W. A. Eddy writes:

> Swift tells us that the Houyhnhnms are more reasonable than Gulliver, but the Houyhnhnms do not bear him out. To me the defect of the fourth voyage is not the brutality of the satire, but the stupidity of the Houyhnhnms, whose judgments of Gulliver prove nothing

beyond their own incompetence to judge. Gulliver is quick to recognize the excellent qualities of the horses. How is it then that the Houyhnhnms, who we are assured are so much more sensible, are unable to recognize that the human body is much more suitable than their own for the common needs of life? . . .

Swift was careless of his story; the fires of misanthropy obscured his judgment, and vitiated his argument. Much may be said for Swift's Yahoo conception of man, but much more against his misconception of the ideal Houyhnhnms. Powerfully as he reiterates and supports his postulate that the horse is the better creature, the Houyhnhnms refute it on every page.

Here Swift and Gulliver are completely identified, regarded as of one mind. Actually, all the postulates are Gulliver's postulates. It is Swift who permits Gulliver to reveal in his narrative the horses' "incompetence to judge."

The most recent attempt to deal with the problem of the fourth voyage is an essay in *Perilous Balance,* by W. B. C. Watkins. Here the solution offered is that the fourth voyage leaves the realms of satire for those of tragedy. The essay is admirable in stressing the profound seriousness and significance of Swift's view of the problem of evil; but in holding that this view is essentially tragic the author misses the demonstrable satiric structure and conclusion of the voyage.

Since no one seems to have had difficulty in reading the first two voyages of *Gulliver* as satire, whence arise the difficulties over the last voyage? One chief source of trouble, I have no doubt, lies outside of Swift and his book, in certain assumptions which are so traditional and conventional that the critic may not only not express them, but may even be unaware of them. It is commonplace to distinguish two modes of satire: the genial, laughing, urbane satire of Horace, and the severe, lashing satire of Juvenal. Whatever hostility the first mode may contain, it nevertheless works largely in terms of laughter. For convenience, it may be termed comic satire. The second mode emphasizes a severely satiric attack in which laughter is at a minimum, or perhaps even lacking. This may be termed caustic or corrosive satire. Swift, like Juvenal, holds a commanding position as a satirist in large part because of the corrosive satire of which he was capable. Yet—and any considerable reading in the history and criticism of satire will support the view —most critics are repelled by corrosive satire and prefer rather to deal with comic satire. I share that preference, indeed, and regard comic satire as a richer, more complete treatment of humanity than purely corrosive satire; but if one unconsciously comes to identify good satire with comic satire only, he is almost certain to have trouble with the fourth voyage of *Gulliver*. Unconsciously expecting the smile or the laugh as a partial balm to severe satiric attack, and finding that this balm is scarcely present in the effective first nine chapters of the last voyage, he may decide that he is no longer reading satire, and hence miss Swift's rounding of the whole of *Gulliver* in a superb return of comic satire.

For we should not assume that, if someone has blundered in the last voyage, the blunderer was therefore Swift. That assumption is dangerously close to the idea that we are superior to Swift because we are superior to Lemuel Gulliver. But Swift paid his readers a higher compliment than most readers will pay him. He assumed, as any ironic satirist by the very nature of his work assumes, that he and his readers were on terms of equality in sharing an important secret, which is that there is far more in literal statement than meets the literal eye. It may be granted that for nine chapters the corrosive satire of the last voyage of *Gulliver* is of unparalleled intensity, and that its recurrent waves are overwhelming enough to swamp minds of considerable displacement, as well as cockleshell intellects. Yet Swift offers us the opportunity to ride out the storm with him, and even goes to some trouble to keep us afloat. If we choose to disregard Swift himself and the last part of Voyage IV, and to go down finally for the third time, with Gulliver, it is hardly Swift's blunder.

II

One of my main concerns here is to show that Gulliver in the last voyage is not Swift. That done, we shall be able to see how Swift, though his corrosive satire continues to the last page of the volume, superadds to it a comic satire of great significance. But our understanding of the last voyage will be made easier if we appreciate certain complex effects achieved by Swift in the earlier voyages. Just as a great composer has a variety of single orchestral instruments which he uses to produce complex music, so Swift has a variety of instruments wherewith he produces the complexity which is *Gulliver's Travels*. Ready to his hand he has the modes of straight narrative, of comedy, of comic satire, and of corrosive satire. And he has the double voice of irony.

Though the voyage to Lilliput is commonly held to be the merriest and most diverting of the four voyages, the greater part of it, quantitatively considered, holds our interest chiefly as ingenious narrative. In the first four chapters, besides a few comic and satiric touches, there is one outstanding passage of comic satire, that concerning the High-Heels and Low-Heels, and the Big-Endians and the Little-Endians. The narrative then resumes chief importance until we reach the end of chapter vi, with its comic passage in which Gulliver defends the reputation of the Lilliputian lady whose name has been scandalously linked with his.

In chapter vii occurs the severest satire of the first voyage. Gulliver, who has deserved the highest gratitude from the Lilliputians, is impeached for capital offenses—chiefly, for making water within the precincts of the burning royal palace "under colour of extinguishing the fire," and for traitorously refusing to reduce the empire of Blefuscu to a province and put to death all the Big-Endian exiles. Though the episode is introduced with a trace of comic absurdity in the articles of impeachment, and in their pompous phrasing, the court's debate on how to dispose of Gulliver is corrosive satire, savage and ironic. It is suggested that Gulliver be put to a painful and ignominious death, his house set on fire, and thousands of poisoned arrows shot into his face and hands. His servants are to strew poisonous juices on his shirt, to make him tear his own flesh and die in the "utmost torture." At this point Reldresal proves himself Gulliver's "true friend" by suggesting that blindness would be a sufficient punishment; but Gulliver's enemies argue against this proposal. His Imperial Majesty, gracious and lenient, holds out against the death sentence, but hints that punishments in addition to blindness may be inflicted on Gulliver. Finally, again through the friendship of Reldresal, it is decided to blind Gulliver and to starve him to death.

In this episode, which is the longest satiric passage in the first voyage and the climax of the voyage, the satiric attack is bitter. As Swift shows the refinements of hypocrisy, ingratitude, and cruelty achieved by the Lilliputian court, mirth leaves him, and he is as severe as in any part of Voyage IV.

Yet the general sense that the voyage is a merry one is sound. The one passage of essentially corrosive satire is largely outweighed by

incidental comedy, by the famous passage of comic satire, and by
the wealth of sheerly narrative detail. By the end of chapter vii the
corrosive attack has ceased—Gulliver is in Blefuscu, lying on the
ground in order to "kiss his Majesty's and the Empress's hand." In
the final chapter he is returned to England, and is in familiar and
kindly surroundings, enjoying the company of his "dear pledges"
and breeding Lilliputian sheep in the absurd hope of improving
the English woolen manufacture. Furthermore, there is the basic
comic absurdity which pervades the entire voyage, namely, Gulliver's attitude in reporting his experiences. Constantly before our
eyes we have the incredible double scale of size, human and Lilliputian, reported without comment by Gulliver, who accepts the
Lilliputian scale as easily as the human. It is the comic incongruity
of inadequate reporting, felt as inadequate when we visualize the
scenes and episodes described by Gulliver. And Swift permits Gulliver so great a use of specific visual detail, in which the two scales
of size are constantly blended, that even the unimaginative reader
has no difficulty in seeing the picture. Thus the scandal about
Gulliver and the Lilliputian lady is immediately comic to the
reader. But as Gulliver goes through his elaborate defense of her
reputation (and his), the comedy is immensely heightened by the
reader's realization of Gulliver's inadequate sense of the situation;
in his long defense he never mentions the one particular that makes
the scandal perfectly absurd, the difference in physical scale.

If one is thinking primarily of the writer, Swift, one may see in
this aspect of Gulliver only a device for understatement. But Swift
is achieving his effects by means of a created character; and we see
that is is not deliberate understatement for Gulliver, it is simply a
result of his character. It is all he finds worth saying. He has definite
limitations of mind, which in spite of his development he never
outgrows, even in the last voyage.

The second voyage, like the first, has much interesting descriptive
and narrative material that is essentially neither comic nor satiric.
But there is an increased proportion of comic episode, and the
corrosive satire carries far more weight than in the first voyage.

The increased comic effect is achieved principally at the expense
of Gulliver, for in the second voyage he is reduced in status and
becomes obviously an object of comic satire. He retains a pride and
self-esteem which would be perfectly normal for him among his
physical equals, but which is ridiculous under the circumstances,

and which results in his being made the comic butt in several episodes. The increased corrosive effect is achieved principally by the long passage wherein Gulliver and the king discuss mankind. To this passage we need to give close attention, for the satiric structure of Voyage IV (although on a different plane) is in important ways parallel to it.

Swift permits Gulliver to give the king a favorable statement about the English system. The king perceives that all is not well with Gulliver's civilization; and being a reasonable, thoughtful monarch, he asks Gulliver a long series of questions. These questions are direct and to the point; the answers, which are obviously called for, show defects in Gulliver's world. In the passage thus far, there is little or no emotional, ironic, or comic effect as the king conducts his grave and judicial inquiry. Finally, when the king has thought over his audiences with Gulliver, he delivers quite calmly his famous criticism of the human race. As he concludes it, he courteously hopes that Gulliver may have escaped many vices of his kind—nevertheless the bulk of humanity is "the most pernicious race of little odious vermin that nature ever suffered to crawl upon the surface of the earth."

So much for the human race, apparently, as judged by a reasonable being who has heard the best case Gulliver can make out for his kind. And the quality is corrosive, not comic. Yet it is only a preliminary to the satire that follows. Gulliver's hope to impress the king has had the reverse effect, but Gulliver himself has not come off badly. Swift now proceeds to allow Gulliver to reveal himself as a typical member of the race, and at the same time drives the satiric attack deeper. Gulliver expresses his great embarrassment at hearing his "noble and most beloved country" so injuriously treated. At this point, and for the first time in the long passage, Swift calls into play the double voice of irony. The squirming Gulliver reveals that he has given "to every point a more favorable turn by many degrees than the strictness of truth would allow"; but nevertheless he condescendingly suggests that "great allowances should be given to a King who lives so wholly secluded from the rest of the world" and hence must have an insufficiency of knowledge and "a certain narrowness of thinking, from which we and the politer countries of Europe are wholly exempted."

Gulliver's comments here have further worsened his case for mankind, besides revealing the absurdity of his sense of superiority to the king. Another satirist might pause at this point, but Swift has still to reach his satiric climax and to reduce Gulliver utterly. Gulliver blunders on: "To confirm what I have now said, and further, to show the miserable effects of a confined education, I shall here insert a passage which will hardly obtain belief." In a word, Gulliver offers the king the secret of gunpowder, giving a notion of its effectiveness by means of a few graphic and specific details. The king is horrified, regards Gulliver as inhuman in advancing such thoughts, and forbids him to mention the matter again. Gulliver is still blind, and shakes his head over the king's reaction, which seems to him "a strange effect of narrow principles and short views."

This long, satiric passage is relatively simple at first, but it becomes elaborate before it ends. We have, first, Gulliver's theme of the excellence of mankind. Next is added the calm and generalized, but corrosive, satire of the king's queries and final dismissal of mankind—a note which sounds through the rest of the passage. Swift then calls irony, and, when he is ready, adds the emotional impact of his most forceful and graphic prose (specific details concerning the effective use of gunpowder). Gulliver's bland assumption that he is doing the king a favor coexists in the reader's mind with the shocking demonstration of what man's inhumanity is capable of; Gulliver is demolishing himself with the reader as well as the king; and Swift is achieving a bitter yet comic irony in Gulliver's naïve unawareness and continued self-assurance. And underlying the whole satiric structure of the long passage is the substructure of physical absurdity: with all his fine words and superiority, Gulliver can be taken into the king's hand and stroked —he is "little Grildrig."

Even so brief an analysis as the foregoing reveals several points important to our discussion. Swift moves from the simpler to the more complex for his satiric climax; to corrosive satire he adds comic and ironic notes. And it is of particular significance to our view of Voyage IV that in achieving his effects Swift has caused Gulliver, unawares, to make a lamentable spectacle of himself.

As we accompany Gulliver to the end of the second voyage, we are in no danger of confusing him with Swift. Gulliver remains likeable—indeed he remains likeable to the end; but Swift always uses him deliberately, even ruthlessly, to further the Swiftian satiric purpose. And Gulliver's characteristics are admirable for this purpose. He is a man of some education, has traveled, and by the end of the second voyage has had very surprising experiences. But he is and remains a type of ordinary, normal man—even a rather simplified version of the type. He is capable with his hands, and quick to meet physical emergency. He is essentially a man of good will, friendly, honest, and ethical according to his lights. His mental make-up is simple and direct, and it permits almost no complexity. He is not torn by any inner conflict, for his psyche is unwilling to admit the diverse possibilities which make for such conflicts. He can be the Gulliver of the first voyage, a man whose normal humanity seems good in the light of petty and ungrateful Lilliputian policy. He can be the Gulliver of the second voyage, whose normal acceptance of the standards and values of his civilization seems bad in the light of largeness and humaneness of spirit. He is much the same man in these two voyages: Swift has shown first the better side of ordinary values, secondly, the worser side. And Gulliver's mind is not at first closed; new experiences occur and give new directions to his thought, or—as in the fourth voyage—produce a shift in his attitude. But the simplicity and naïveté remain; his mind is a single-track one. It never compasses the complex and the contradictory; it cleaves to the best line it knows, but to that line alone.

That Gulliver's mind is not at first closed, but yet is limited, has important consequences. Thus, while he is open-minded, he can change from one attitude to another under the pressure of what he sees and hears about him. Although always a giant in Lilliput, he adopts easily the prevailing Lilliputian scale. Although he is miniature in Brobdingnag, being completely surrounded by a gigantic environment he comes to take the gigantic scale as normal. That new attitude having become habitual with him, the fact of his own minuteness (though constant to his experience) drops out of his mind and ceases to have any meaning. And his new, oversimplified attitude has a narrowness and rigidity which continues after he leaves the land of the giants, and results in comedy when he returns to a world built to his scale. Back in England, he says, "I was afraid of trampling on every traveller I met, and often called aloud to have them stand out of the way, so that I had like to have gotten one or two broken heads for my impertinence." He behaves so unaccountably toward his family that they conclude he has lost his wits. In effect, his new attitude prevents him from believing the evidence of his own eyes. But his mind is not closed, and gradually

the physical realities recall him to a proper sense of scale. On
Voyage IV, however, in the simple intellectual and moral environment of the Houyhnhnms, and horrified at the Yahoos, Gulliver has
that final intellectual development and illumination which leads to
the completely closed mind. It is a situation which permits Swift
to develop his corrosive attack, but we ought not be surprised to
find that Swift remains superior to his puppet to the end, and
reveals an attitude different from Gulliver's.

III

The first two voyages of *Gulliver* are two complementary parts
which make up one large unit of satire. The fourth part of the book
is not simply an additional voyage, more severely satirical but on
the whole to be read like the earlier voyages; it is a voyage different
in concept and in treatment, and hence it is not to be judged by
the same criteria.

We notice at once that the fourth voyage lacks the picturesque
and interesting descriptive and narrative detail so abundantly present in the earlier voyages. There is, for instance, no double physical
scale, and there is little narrative action. Swift does, of course,
embody the chief elements of his satiric analysis in the concrete
symbols of the horse and the Yahoo, and he describes the Yahoo in
full and unpleasant detail. Even so, the spirit and scheme of the
fourth voyage employ far less narrative richness than is expended
on Lilliput and Brobdingnag, since Swift shifts the emphasis of his
attack. The satire of the earlier voyages is concerned with the flaws
and defects of man's actions. Voyage IV cuts deeper. Actions and
doings are symptomatic of man's nature—the corrosive satire of the
last voyage is concerned with the springs and causes of action, in
other words, with the inner make-up of man. Hence, though there
is a narrative thread in Voyage IV, and considerable detail about
the Yahoo, the voyage is characterized less by fullness of narrative
than by fullness of analysis.

Another difference in the fourth voyage should be noted. Here
the reader himself is inescapably an object of satiric attack. In the
first voyage he may remain calm in the face of the satire. There is
not only a good deal else to divert his attention; there is also the
fact that the activities of monarchs and statesmen are the actions of

an exceedingly small group of people. The reader's withers are un-wrung. He may even remain relatively detached emotionally in reading of Gulliver's offer of gunpowder to the Brobdingnagian king. After all, war has been so far only an intermittent activity of nations, and the reader probably disapproves of it in theory as much as Swift does. But the reader cannot evade the attack in the last voyage: Swift is attacking the Yahoo in each of us.

Furthermore, it has now become Swift's purpose to drive home the satire, insistently and relentlessly. Had he wished to achieve only the diverting and comic satire of Voyages I and II, with occa-sional touches of the severer sort, he need not have written the last voyage. But he chose to go on, and in the fourth voyage corrosive satire at last comes home deeply and profoundly to his readers. In truth, the constant protests against it are evidence of its effectiveness.

Mere narrative or comic detail concerning either the Yahoos or the Houyhnhnms would inevitably tend to weaken, divert, or block off the intensity of the attack; hence Swift makes little use of such detail. He sharply cuts human nature into two parts. He gives reason and benevolence to the Houyhnhnms. Unrestrained and selfish appetites, and a mere brutish awareness, are left for the Yahoo. Since he is writing satire rather than panegyric, the good qualities are given the nonhuman form of the horse, and the bad qualities the nearly human form of the Yahoo. Consider how much less effective the satire would have been had the Houyhnhnms been merely a superior human race—the reader would naturally evade the satiric attack by identifying himself as a Houyhnhnm. Again, for intensity of attack, Swift dwells with unpleasant particularity on Yahoo form and nature: the emphasis is necessarily on Yahoo form and nature. In this connection, it should be said that the un-pleasant physical characteristics of the Yahoos are in themselves hardly as repellent as the disgusting physical details Gulliver has noted among the Brobdingnagians. The microscopic eye among the giants produces perhaps as repulsive a series of physical images as can be found in literature; but, for all that, we are aware of a fantastic enlargement, and this makes for relative unreality. The Yahoos are not giants, they resemble us all too closely in some ways, and their unpleasant physical traits are displayed to us without the variety of relief permitted in Voyage II.

Swift's aim in the last voyage is to spare us nothing. If we could chuckle and laugh at the Yahoos, or be diverted by their activities,

by so much would Swift have weakened his corrosive satire. And
the same exigency governs his treatment of the Houyhnhnms. To
make much of them for comic or narrative effect would impair
Swift's chief purpose.

One further point: In the first nine chapters of Voyage IV, Swift
further simplifies and concentrates his attack by making almost no
use of irony; the attack on Yahoo-man is not only severe, but literal
and direct.

Is the misanthropy of the fourth voyage, then, too much to accept? Is Swift's hatred all-consuming? Has it abandoned itself to
wanton and animus-ridden insult? Has the sanity of his rich and
complex genius been dissipated? Before we agree with the many
who have answered "Yes" to such questions, let us contemplate the
voyage as a whole. For Swift not only wrote the first nine chapters
of Voyage IV; he also wrote the last three. To neglect these final
chapters is like ignoring the final couplet in a Shakespearean sonnet,
the last part of a tragi-comedy like *The Winter's Tale*, or the last
three chapters of *Moby Dick*. It is true that Swift's final attitude
may not be obvious to a superficial reader, or to one inhibited
(perhaps unconsciously) from reading *Gulliver* as a complete satire.
But great and complex artists usually make some demands on their
readers, and Swift is no exception. *Gulliver's Travels* is easier to understand than *A Tale of a Tub*; but it by no means follows that
Lemuel Gulliver's naïve and simple misanthropy can be equated
with the sophisticated satirist who recounted Gulliver's adventures.
One should be on guard against simplifying an elaborate ironist.

Swift himself has warned us, if we are at all wary. To say that
the first nine chapters of the fourth voyage are almost continuous
corrosive satire is not to say that there are not some narrative and
comic touches. Swift obviously visualized the Houyhnhnms very
definitely as horses. It must have been a temptation to his constructive and comic imagination not to avail himself of the opportunities
offered by the horse form. Generally he restrains himself: thus
Gulliver remembers once seeing some Houyhnhnms "employed in
domestic business," but he does not specify what business. Yet Swift
cannot resist an occasional bit of fun at the expense of the Houyhnhnms. They have an absolute self-assurance in the completeness of
their knowledge and experience. The etymology of the word
Houyhnhnm means "horse," but also "the perfection of nature."
Their intellectual limitations and arrogance are divertingly illus-

trated in the passage wherein the Houyhnhnm criticizes the human form. In every point wherein man and horse differ, the Houyhnhnm automatically and even absurdly assumes that the advantage lies obviously with the horse; for example, that four legs are better than two, or that the human anatomy is defective since Gulliver cannot eat without lifting one of his "fore feet" to his mouth. While Swift, in pursuit of his purpose, is chary of making the horses absurd, there are enough comic touches to guard the attentive reader from assuming that Swift accepts Gulliver's worshipful attitude toward the horses.

Further evidence that Swift was well aware that the Houyhnhnms were, after all, horses, and that they offered more material for comedy than he had permitted himself to use in his text, may be found in a letter he wrote his publisher, Motte, concerning illustrations for a new edition of the *Travels*. Since he tells Motte that a return of his deafness has put him "in an ill way to answer a letter which requires some thinking," and since the letter also indicates that he has not reread *Gulliver* but is trusting to memory, it may be presumed that his remarks indicate his normal attitude toward the book. The relevant part of his letter reads:

> The Country of Horses, I think, would furnish many [occasions for illustration]. Gulliver brought to be compared with the Yahoos; the family at dinner and he waiting; the grand council of horses, assembled, sitting, one of them standing with a hoof extended, as if he were speaking; the she-Yahoo embracing Gulliver in the river, who turns away his head in disgust; the Yahoos got into a tree, to infest him under it; the Yahoos drawing carriages, and driven by a horse with a whip in his hoof. I can think of no more, but Mr. Gay will advise you.

Swift's suggestions for illustrations, added to the few ludicrous suggestions in the first nine chapters of the fourth voyage, indicate that he took as a matter of course that there was a certain amount of comic effect in the rather simple horses visualized in their relationship of superiority to Gulliver and the Yahoos. Since Gulliver's Houyhnhnm worship is a vital element in making the corrosive attack on Yahoo nature effective, it might seem that Swift had bungled his craft in permitting even slight evidences of the limitations of the Houyhnhnms. Actually, without weakening the main attack of the early part of the voyage, these slight hints foreshadow

Swift's attitude in the last three chapters. As a composer of music, giving almost complete emphasis to a main theme, may suggest from time to time a new theme before he develops it fully, so Swift, while developing misanthropic and corrosive satire at length, hints from time to time at another theme.

The horses and Gulliver have it all their own way for the first nine chapters of the last voyage. Yahoo-man has been presented in all his horror; Swift has achieved the most blasting and unrelieved satiric attack possible, and at great length. What simple and indignant reason can say against the flaws and defects of human nature has been said, and said exhaustively. Gulliver's revolt against his kind is so complete that Swift is able to give the knife a final twist: mankind is, if anything, worse than the Yahoo, since man is afflicted by pride, and makes use of what mental power he has to achieve perversions and corruptions undreamed of by the Yahoo.

At this point of the satiric attack many readers have ceased really to read the book, and have concluded that this was Swift's final word because it is Gulliver's final word. Swept away by the force of the corrosive attack on Yahoo-man, they conclude that Gulliver is at last Swift. (Such a misconception is facilitated no doubt by Swift's temporary abandonment of irony for straightforward invective.) In the last three chapters, however, Swift shows that Gulliver's word cannot be final.

Swift, satirist and realist, is well aware that there is more of the Yahoo in humanity than there is of benevolence and reason. And he develops his attack as forcibly as he can, by means of corrosive satire, in terms of pessimism and misanthropy. But this is only a part of Swift. He is also perfectly aware that the problem is not so simply solved as it is for the Houyhnhnms and for Gulliver. He knows that there is much to be hated in the animal called man, but he knows also that there are individuals whom he loves. The horses have no room for anything between Houyhnhnm and Yahoo, and Gulliver takes over this too simple attitude. Just as his physical sense of proportion was upset by his voyage to the country of the giants, so here his intellectual sense of proportion is overbalanced. The limited, simplified Houyhnhnm point of view is obviously better to him than the Yahoo state; and he cleaves to it. Swift can keep clear the double physical scale of Gulliver and giant; not so, Gulliver. Swift can differentiate between Yahoo and Gulliver, and does—but Gulliver himself is convinced he is a Yahoo. The attentive reader will realize that Gulliver is the one actual human being present through the first nine blighting chapters of the last voyage. Hence he is not only a constant reminder that horse and Yahoo are symbols, but also a constant demonstration that a human being is not a Yahoo.

Swift has fun with Gulliver in chapter x. Gulliver has finally come to the conclusion that human beings are, if anything, worse than Yahoos. As much as possible he tries to transform himself into a horse:

> By conversing with the Houyhnhnms, and looking upon them with delight, I fell to imitate their gait and gesture, which is now grown into a habit, and my friends often tell me in a blunt way, that I trot like a horse; which, however, I take for a great compliment. Neither shall I disown that in speaking I am apt to fall into the voice and manner of the Houyhnhnms . . .

And in the paragraph immediately following this excerpt, with Gulliver at the height of his enchantment, Swift has the horses, with more ruthlessness than benevolence, order Gulliver to leave the island and swim back to the place whence he came. Gulliver swoons. He is allowed two months to finish a boat, and is granted the assistance of a sorrel nag, who "had a tenderness" for him. It is a diverting picture: Gulliver and the sorrel nag working away together to make a canoe, "covering it with the skins of Yahoos well stitched together" and "stopping all the chinks with Yahoos' tallow." When the moment of parting comes:

> His Honor, out of curiosity and perhaps (if I may speak it without vanity) partly out of kindness, was determined to see me in my canoe. . . . I took a second leave of my master; but as I was going to prostrate myself to kiss his hoof, he did me the honor to raise it gently to my mouth. I am not ignorant how much I have been censured for mentioning this last particular. For my detractors are pleased to think it improbable that so illustrious a person should descend to give so great a mark of distinction to a creature so inferior as I. . . .
> My master and his friends continued on the shore till I was almost out of sight; and I often heard the sorrel nag (who always loved me) crying out, *Hnuy illa nyha majah Yahoo,* Take care of thyself, gentle Yahoo.

It is heartbreaking for Gulliver; but for Swift and the reader it is not wholly a matter for tears.

Gulliver's design is to make his way to an "uninhabited island," but he is evenutally found by the crew of a Portuguese ship. Gulliver's meeting with the crew returns him to the real world; he is no longer the sole representative of humanity, placed between horse and Yahoo. In the earlier voyages, Swift had spent only a few pages on Gulliver's return to the real world; in the last, he gives two chapters to it. Those chapters deserve very careful reading: they are, as the book now stands, the climax of Swift's whole satire as well as the end of the fourth voyage. Gulliver, hating himself and all men as Yahoos, is reintroduced to the world of actual men and women. What happens? If Swift's view is the same as Gulliver's, he ought to go on with his severe satire against mankind, now even deepening it with specific examples of Yahoo nature. He does nothing of the sort. Rather, he shows us very carefully and at some length the insufficiency of Gulliver's new attitude. Gulliver continues to "tremble between fear and hatred" when confronted by human beings, while at the same time his own account of affairs shows that the persons with whom he comes into contact are essentially honest, kindly, and generous. It is the same limited mentality in Gulliver which has been noted in previous voyages. He has adopted a final rigid and oversimplified attitude, which so completely possesses him that he cannot believe the evidence of his own experience; since he now sees man only as Yahoo, he cannot even take in contradictory evidence when faced with it.

The Portuguese crew speak to Gulliver "with great humanity" when they find him; but he is horrified. Concluding that his misfortunes have "impaired his reason" (as indeed they have), they deliver him up to the captain.

> [The captain's] name was Pedro de Mendez; he was a very courteous and generous person; he entreated me to give some account of myself, and desired to know what I would eat and drink; said I should be used as well as himself, and spoke so many obliging things, that I wondered to find such civilities in a Yahoo. However, I remained silent and sullen; I was ready to faint at the very smell of him and his men.

Gulliver finally promises the captain not to attempt anything against his own life, but at the same time protests that he will "suffer the greatest hardships rather than return to live among Yahoos." In the course of the voyage home, out of gratitude to Don Pedro, Gulliver sometimes sits with the captain and tries to conceal his antipathy to mankind. The captain offers Gulliver the best suit of clothes he has; Gulliver will accept only two clean shirts, which, he thinks, will not so much "defile" him. In Lisbon, the captain still further aids Gulliver, takes him into his house, and persuades him to accept a newly made suit of clothes. Gulliver finds that his terror at humanity gradually lessens: the captain's "whole deportment was so obliging, added to a very good *human* understanding, that I really began to tolerate his company." But though the terror might lessen, Gulliver's "hatred and contempt seemed to increase."

Why does Swift give us Don Pedro, the kindly, generous individual? Obviously as a foil to Gulliver's misanthropy, as evidence that Gulliver has gone off the deep end and cannot recover himself from the nightmare view of Yahoo-man. Chapter xi is almost wholly a demonstration that Gulliver is absurd in his blind refusal to abandon his misanthropic convictions. His conduct upon his return home is the ultimate result of his aberration. His family receive him with joy, but the sight of them fills Gulliver with hatred, contempt, and disgust. When his wife kisses him, he falls "into a swoon for almost an hour." His adopted attitude of mind, directed by the too simple Houyhnhnm view, permits him to see only the Yahoo in man or woman. Even after five years he will not permit any member of his family to take him by the hand. But we may allow him to characterize his mode of life himself:

> The first money I laid out was to buy two young stone-horses, which I kept in a good stable, and next to them the groom is my greatest favorite, for I feel my spirits revived by the smell he contracts in the stable. My horses understand me tolerably well; I converse with them at least four hours every day.

Gulliver's attitude is not the solution, and Swift knew it. It is too unbalanced and unrealistic for a final attitude, and Swift presents its absurdity—so clearly as to make one wonder how he could have been so misunderstood. Gulliver's attitude is in effect a complete quarrel with man, a final refusal to accept the nature of mankind. To charge Swift with the same final refusal is to ignore the evidence. In this connection a passage from the second voyage

where surely Swift is speaking through Gulliver, is helpful. Gulliver
has been reading a Brobdingnagian book, and says:

> This writer went through all the usual topics of European moralists,
> showing how diminutive, contemptible, and helpless was man in his
> own nature [i.e., the sixty-foot nature of the Brobdingnagians]. . . .
> The author drew several moral applications useful in the conduct of
> life, but needless here to repeat. For my own part, I could not avoid
> reflecting how universally this talent was spread, of drawing lectures
> in morality, or indeed matter for discontent and repining, from the
> quarrels we raise with nature.

I do not by any means wish to say that Swift was always superior
to drawing matter for discontent and repining from quarrels raised
with nature. He was clear-sighted and sensitive; he was an ethical
moralist and a satirist. Much in the nature of man was hateful and
detestable to him, and he often attacked it and quarreled with it
in no uncertain terms. But, though Gulliver's soul was completely
discontented, completely repining, Swift could rise to a far higher
plane, and did so. Swift was much more than a corrosive satirist
only; he had a high sense of the comic, and in the final satiric vision
of the concluding chapters of *Gulliver* the Gulliverian discontent
is supplemented by, and enclosed in, comic satire, with Gulliver
himself as the butt.

In Voyage IV, Swift gives his severest satiric vision full scope, but
knows that conclusions growing out of this nightmare vision are
inadequate and invalid. He lets Gulliver go the whole horse, and
up to the last page the negative, corrosive attack is present. But
what else he does in those last chapters is unique in the history of
satiric literature: the severe attack with its apparently rational basis
and its horrifying conclusions continues to the end in the personal
narrative of Swift's puppet. Thus severe satire remains the main
theme, but the new theme of Gulliver's absurdity complicates the
issue. By rising to a larger and more comprehensive view than he
permits to Gulliver, Swift is satirically commenting on the insufficiency of the corrosive attitude. The evils in the world and in man
are such that it is no wonder that a simple and ethical nature may
be driven to despair and misanthropy. Nevertheless, such an attitude
Swift demonstrates to be inadequate and absurd.

Gulliver's attitude, in its simplicity and finality, is a kind of
misanthropic solution of the problem of evil. It is a tempting solu-

tion for a severe satirist; but Swift found it too limited and too unreal. So far as I can see, Swift offers no answer of his own, no solution. But he does transcend the misanthropic solution. He could see that his own severest satire was the result of a partial and one-sided view, which was therefore properly a subject for mirth.

This seems to me the final comedy of Lemuel Gulliver—that Swift could make an elaborate and subtle joke at the expense of a very important part of himself. We may leave Lemuel in amiable discourse in the stable, inhaling the grateful odor of horse. But Swift is not with him, Swift is above him in the realm of comic satire, still indignant at the Yahoo in man, but at the same time smiling at the absurdity of the view that can see *only* the Yahoo in man.

Situational Satire:

A Commentary on the Method of Swift

by Ricardo Quintana

I

Much depends on the readiness with which we acknowledge the element of impersonality in literary art. The impersonality of drama we perceive and accept instinctively, since our normal responses to a play are grounded in this very acceptance. We do not confuse the dramatist with his characters; unless we are Romantic critics writing on Shakespeare, we do not take the play as direct expression of the writer's personality. The play stands forth as an artifice; we are willing to think of it and discuss it in terms of structural form. How different in this respect our reactions are to most nondramatic forms of literary art can be measured by the degree to which we confound the writer and the written work. When we see the work and its author as interchangeable, when we take the work to be an act at the level of everyday behavior, we have pretty well lost sight of the impersonal element and the presence of anything in the nature of deliberate method and form. For such reasons we often find it hard to come to terms with the lyric poem as a poem, as a construct, with the result that much of our commentary on poetry turns out to be either description of our impressions or reconstruction—largely imaginary—of a precise moment in the poet's emotional history with which we have chosen to equate the poem. Perhaps we find it hardest of all to

"Situational Satire: A Commentary on the Method of Swift," by Ricardo Quintana. From *The University of Toronto Quarterly*, XVII (1948), 130-136. Reprinted by permission of the author and *The University of Toronto Quarterly*.

admit of any distinction between a satirist and his satiric composition—and this despite the fact that satire is much more obviously a form of rhetoric than is lyric poetry. It is scarcely surprising, therefore, that Swift's satiric method, which everywhere stares us in the face, is only dimly recognized to be a method. We praise Swift's style; we speak of his use of allegory and his mastery of disgust; but we do not follow through with conviction. Sooner or later we allow the personality of Swift to take over and in consequence to obscure the artist, the craftsman, who after all is only Jonathan Swift's distant relative.

It is perfectly apparent—and here is a key that will unlock the first door—that in every one of Swift's more notable prose satires we have a fictional character or group of characters: Lemuel Gulliver; Isaac Bickerstaff; M. B. Drapier; the humanitarian projector who writes *A Modest Proposal;* the three brothers in the *Tale of a Tub.* What we refuse to see is that Swift himself is *not* present, that it is the characters who are in complete charge. Swift's method is uniformly by way of dramatic satire. He creates a fully realized character and a fully realized world for him to move in. Sometimes, as in *Gulliver's Travels,* the satiric action is developed in terms of the character's reactions to this world; but frequently the action is of essentially another sort, deriving from the crazy assurance with which the character makes himself at home in his cloud-cuckoo-land, tidies the place up, and proceeds to enlarge the bounds of his estate. The difference referred to is a real one, a genuine difference of method, something much more ponderable than the words which must be used to describe it. It is the difference between Gulliver and Bickerstaff, between the *Travels* and the Partridge-Bickerstaff Papers. Gulliver is a reluctant explorer, cast by storms and tides upon strange countries where he is compelled to live at the mercy of the inhabitants. Isaac Bickerstaff, by contrast, is at the mercy of nothing: he assumes such complete control over the laws of logic and astrology that he does not hesitate to condemn a man to death and carry out the sentence.

The latter method is more characteristic of Swift than the method employed in *Gulliver's Travels.* Both are dramatic in the sense suggested, consisting of the depiction of characters and worlds, the character being sometimes projected into a world prepared for him in advance, but more often being allowed to create one for himself. It is in regard to the character's creation of his own world that we begin to suspect that something more than what we ordinarily think of as a dramatic method has perhaps entered into the compositions of Swift. In the *Tale of a Tub* we hear of "many famous discoveries, projects, and machines," of noteworthy devices, of arts highly useful to the commonwealth. In point of fact, the entire *Tale* and its accompanying *Discourse concerning the Mechanical Operation of the Spirit* are one long series of projects, devices, and machines, spun out with amazing bravura. What was there about projectors and projects that so fascinated this particular satiric artist?

II

Before pressing on in further search of Swift's satiric method, we ought perhaps to establish our larger view. The misinterpretation of Swift is proverbial, but with fewer exceptions than is sometimes realized those who have written about him have fought energetically against the deep-lying prejudices of the sort voiced so deplorably and so brilliantly by Thackeray. It happens that we know a good deal of both the private life of Swift and his public career, and much about his motives, interests, prejudices, and theoretical convictions. Criticism, as distinct from biography, is concerned to find the relationship between the man and the artist, but this it can do to some degree of effectiveness only through a sense of the general problem. How do the writer as man and the writer as artist stand to one another? Where does personality end and impersonality begin?

Satire, as much as and no less than drama and lyric poetry, is a construct. It is precisely devised literary composition, a form of rhetoric. It may proceed, as we have seen, by way of characters whose actions are recorded objectively or who speak as in a play; but even in the absence of such ikons there is still the assumed character of the satirist, which despite a convincingly deceptive egotism is quite as much an imaginative creation as any ikon. Nor, in another and more vital respect, is there any substantial difference between satire on the one hand and drama and lyric poetry on the other. Each of these fashions its own world, not as Swift creates the land of the Houyhnhnms or Shakespeare the island of Prospero, but rather in the sense that *Gulliver's Travels*—all of it—is a world, that *The Tempest*—the play as a totality—is its own, complete universe.

This governs feeling and speech. It is at once a way of looking at things, a way of feeling, and a way of speaking.

The writer himself, the man with a human character and practical motives, is present of course, but he stands several levels away from this manner of feeling and speech. The avowed intention of the satirist is to expose folly and evil and to castigate them, and there is no satire worthy of the name which does not in fact establish a moral dichotomy: right over against wrong, rectified vision or virtue against twisted vision, human dignity and freedom against stupidity, blindness, perversity. If the moral sense of some satirists —of Byron, for instance—seems elementary, the moral sense of Swift we recognize as that inherited from the humanist tradition, in which man's freedom was defined in terms of ethical responsibility and in accord with the Christian awareness of human incapacity and failure. The drift of Swift's satiric statements, their intellectual-ethical significance, the practical effects they were designed to achieve are made clear by the history of the age and our knowledge of Swift's character. The impact of his satires is another problem, for their meaning as satiric constructs embraces something which is more than their practical meaning and qualitatively different from it. What this other thing is, is the question, or rather, how to find the terms which will enable us to talk about it without evasion. It is a way of thought and feeling, but only as it is a method —a tone, a style, a manner of execution—can it be described in the language which criticism must come to when it seeks to put close observation in the place of impressionism.

III

It is essential to sense the fact that the method of Swift is a good deal more than what we often think of as a method. Fundamentally, it is an imaginative point of view, making possible and controlling a kind of translation into terms peculiar to a certain angle of perception. This means that it cannot be exclusively identified with any single procedure or device however characteristic of Swift. Though dramatic construction marks all of his best-known satiric works, it would be a mistake to regard such construction as the gist of the matter. Similarly, we have to resist any temptation to single out Swift's use of allegory or of parody in an effort to isolate his method. All of these devices operate together; they are modes of expression within a single language; they are functions of something larger. What name we find for this enclosing method is not particularly important, since there is no precise term that can do all the necessary work. *Situational satire* will serve.

A satire of Swift's is, we may say, an exhibited situation or series of such situations. Once the situation has been suggested, once its tone, its flavor have been given, it promptly takes command of itself and proceeds to grow and organize by virtue of its own inherent principles. It is a state of affairs within which, as we mistakenly put it, "anything can happen"—mistakenly because everything that does happen is instantly recognized as a part of *this*, a unique situation. Nevertheless, the room for self-improvisation seems limitless, and the comic scale ranges from the hilarious to the grim. It is to be observed that the satirist is himself not involved: he is as much an observer, as much outside all the fuss and nonsense, as we are. (Is it this that we mean when, in speaking of the satires, we comment on the "coldness of Swift"? We know that he was not cold, else we should not be quoting his epitaph as we do.) For the incidents which come to pass no one can be held responsible, any more than for the ideas and emotions which appear. What we have is, literally, an exhibition: everything is shown; everything is at least one degree removed from reality. In short, the situation may be thought of as a kind of chamber within which ideas and emotions are made to move and collide at accelerated speed.

With a recognition of the situation as such comes a perception of the functional character of Swift's favorite devices, which serve both in the creation of the situation and in the generation of the kinetic energy by which it is sustained. There are at least five of these devices that strike us forcibly: drama by way of created characters; parody, or at any rate the imitation of a specific literary *genre*; allegory; the "myth"; and "discoveries, projects, and machines." Of the first of these enough has already been said. Nor is it necessary to dwell at length on Swift's use of parody; we find epic parody in the closing passages of the *Battle*, parody of modern scribblers throughout the *Tale*, parody of the projector's pamphlet in the *Modest Proposal*, and the faithful reproduction, in *Gulliver's Travels*, of the style, tone, and matter-of-fact reporting found in the genuine travel books of the time. Parody is in itself so close to the dramatic method that the two are sometimes difficult to distinguish; in Swift, parody is only another means of creating and exploiting a situation having its own unmistakable thickness. The world which the *Modest Proposal* invites us to live in is our own familiar world twice refracted, our world as remade in the enthusiastic imagination of a typical projector, and that remade world further distorted through parody.

Allegory in Swift's satires is really of two sorts. When it sets up a recognizable parallelism between two systems of events or ideas it derives quite directly from the kind of allegory which was constantly being used by post-Restoration writers in commenting on contemporary events. The political allegory running through *Gulliver's Travels* is of this nature. Much the same are the short fable (the spider-bee episode in the *Battle*) and the extended fable (the story of the animated books in the *Battle* and the story of the three brothers in the *Tale*). The whole point of allegory thus employed lies in clear correspondence, one set of details suggesting and interpreting another set. But if we agree that the *Mechanical Operation of the Spirit* is "by way of allegory," we find ourselves confronted by something that does not fully answer to this kind of running parallelism. In this latter satiric fragment, attached to the *Tale* and the *Battle*, we are reminded that Mahomet refused fiery chariots, winged horses, and celestial sedans, and "would be borne to Heaven upon nothing but his ass"; and to go on "by way of allegory," we are asked to use, for the term *ass*, that of *gifted* or *enlightened teacher* and for *rider, fanatic auditory*. In this case, it seems, almost any parallelism no matter how fantastic will serve, since what is required is only an initial correspondence. The "allegory" does not throw light; rather, it is a challenge in response to which there arises a crazy world where religious fervor is created by mechanical means. And even where Swift is using allegory for sustained correspondence, one sometimes observes that the emerging situation tends to assert its independence. In the *Tale of a Tub*, for instance, the allegorical base on which the story of the three brothers rests never drops from sight, but with Peter and again with Jack we have an exuberant and perverted sense of power, of capacity to improvise and invent, which though in accord with the religious allegory is altogether in excess of it.

What have been called Swift's "myths" are familiar to every reader of the satires. Thus, it is the animal myth which informs both the

Modest Proposal and the fourth book of *Gulliver's Travels*. Others appear in the *Tale of a Tub*, giving us that sect who worship tailors because of a belief that the universe is a large suit of clothes, the Aeolists who affirm "the gift of belching to be the noblest act of a rational creature," and the philosophical system which holds that all notable achievements are the result of madness. The Hobbian myth is of frequent occurrence: a set of principles, a practical program, worked out from the assumption that man is a physical mechanism, his acts a phase not of intelligence but solely of matter. It is this kind of systematized make-believe, a nonsensical "as is," that gives life to the latter part of Gulliver's description of the Grand Academy of Lagado (Book III, chapter VI), where we are told of that school of political projectors whose admirable practices result from a clear understanding of the strict universal resemblance between the natural and the political body.

In what sense are these expanded metaphors to be taken as myths? The distinctive character of Swift's intuition, of his imaginative grasp of the human dilemma, is a moral realism which renounces with superb pride any mythological vision of human destiny. Only the fool believes he can see better through colored glasses. The burden of civilization can be borne solely by such as have learned that human dignity is achieved not through hope but through willful disillusion, acceptance, resolution. If one sought to be paradoxical, one could say that the only myth genuinely embraced by Swift is the myth that there are no myths, the myth for which he found many statements, all of them variants of the single theme of the outside vs. the inside. "Last week I saw a woman flayed, and you will hardly believe how much it altered her person for the worse." This moral realism, emphasizing so mordantly and so insistently the deceptive fairness of the surface in contrast with what lies inside, was with Swift a passionate belief. Its metaphorical expressions, however, are less in the nature of myths than antimyths, being in fact a kind of parody with a grim and earnest purpose. As statements they are designed to narrow, to shrink, not to enlarge.

The myths previously referred to (the Hobbian myth, etc.) are clearly of the fantastic order, and often blend into those "discoveries, projects, and machines" of which so much is said in the satires. Indeed, what for the projector himself is a cherished myth is for us an antimyth, a machine, art, or device concocted in that madhouse which is the enthusiast's brain. The myth and the project, no less than dramatic form, parody, and allegory, are means whereby situations are brought about.

IV

That the method we have been speaking of appears for the first time in the great satire published in 1704, comprising the *Tale,* the *Battle,* and the *Mechanical Operation,* and not at all in the earlier Pindaric odes, written during the first years at Moor Park, is perhaps a sufficient reminder that Swift attained artistic maturity when he discovered and put on a hitherto unknown personality, a nonself who spoke and therefore thought a new idiom. The assurance which marks every passage of the 1704 satire is of one who has found creative freedom by learning how to avoid direct participation. The comedy of ideas, the self-developing irony of the situation require no intervention. Yet somehow, in this comedy that enacts itself and improvises its own language, Swift's passionate intuition has found its proper form.

Though each of the satires included in the 1704 volume is in itself an unmistakable comedy, we must not miss the larger comedy presented by the book as a whole, which by bringing the *Tale,* the *Battle of the Books,* and the *Mechanical Operation* into forced relationship establishes a context within which the three pieces are to be construed. Everything about them, the forms they are cast in, the deplorable gaps in the text, the marginal notes, the impertinence with which they ask to be taken as a trilogy, is part of this inclusive situation.

From this time on the method so brilliantly sustained in *A Tale of a Tub* becomes a part of Swift. It is his *alter ego,* his personality as prose satirist. Seen from the outside (how else can analysis view it?) it is method at the lower level of stratagem, and Swift knew he had fashioned something in the way of comic technique. "There is one thing," he wrote in the "Apology" (1710) for the *Tale,* "which the judicious reader cannot but have observed, that some of those passages in this discourse . . . are what they call parodies, where the author personates the style and manner of other writers, whom he has a mind to expose." That it is far more than technique, that it is imagination and intuition, we acknowledge consciously or otherwise through our response to the satiric work of Swift taken as a whole—consciously when we recognize the presence of the artist, instinctively when we think we see a soul writhing in indignation.

Because the method of Swift is more than anything else a creative perception it cannot be summarized. Its essence is its history, its occurrence under different modes in the satires which came to be written. It operates in one fashion in *Gulliver's Travels,* notably in Books I, II, and IV (the comparative ineffectiveness of the third book being attributable to a relaxation of the method save in those passages concerning the virtuosi and the Struldbrugs). We can find it in the Drapier Letters: "They say 'Squire C—y has *Sixteen Thousand Pounds a Year,* now if he sends for the *Rent* to Town, as it is likely he does, he must have *Two Hundred and Forty Horses* to bring up his *Half Years Rent. . . .*" There is nothing to stop such ready calculation, and we shortly find ourselves with £40,000 and 1,200 horses on our hands. Leslie Stephen, speaking with the gravity of a cabinet minister, took exception to the economic heresies which gave rise to such arithmetic. But the Drapier was right, after all. Walpole and Wood were forcing on Ireland a monetary situation that was preposterous. The Drapier's inspired vision of a team of 1,200 horses drawing £40,000—all in copper halfpennies—about the streets of Dublin was no mere Irish myth.

Two final instances of the method. *An Argument against Abolishing Christianity* can perhaps be adequately described as ironic disputation. However, it is disputation that is more than a colloquy between A (who views abolition with concern) and B (all who, for various reasons, would abolish). A is likewise a multiplicity of voices, each point of view that is pressed into service carrying with it a somewhat different personality. It is a dialogue between the speaker's various selves, each of whom has a myth wherewith to confound his adversary; the full pattern of the "argument" emerges solely from eccentric points of reference.

If the *Argument* is Erasmian (and Platonic), *A Modest Proposal* is pure Swift. Nowhere else is the method clearer, nowhere else is the fusion of moral insight and imaginative translation so complete. It is a character in action, a parody, a project, and an animal myth all at once, a situation within which any distinction between art and propaganda seems meaningless.

Swift: The Dean as Satirist

by Ernest Tuveson

It is now generally recognized that the fourth voyage of *Gulliver's Travels,* far from being the expression of a psychopathic hate for mankind, embodies a deep and by no means wholly pessimistic conviction about the place of man and the meaning of his existence in the universe. It is, as Miss Kathleen M. Williams has pointed out, the culmination of "Swift's lifelong attack on the pride of man, especially the pride which convinces him that he can live by the light of unaided reason." [1] She notes that men "stand apart from the two races of this animal world, separated from both by characteristics of which neither the naturally virtuous and rational animals, nor the vicious and irrational ones have any knowledge. . . ."

What has not been fully defined hitherto is the *rationale* of this situation. In what faith is it fixed, and how did Swift come to such opinions? What, exactly, is the position of the Houyhnhnms—why, as Miss Williams points out, do they strike us as somehow cold and even repellent? Is there here some artistic failure of Swift? If they are intended to represent a "satiric norm" against which human beings are contrasted, they fail in their function, for they do not win our allegiance. Again, how are we to account for the final comedy of Gulliver, when the mariner returns home for the last time, with an almost unconquerable aversion to even the best of his own species? It would appear that this episode leaves us with a

"Swift: The Dean as Satirist," by Ernest Tuveson. From *The University of Toronto Quarterly,* XXII (1953), 368-375. Reprinted by permission of *The University of Toronto Quarterly.*

[1] "Gulliver's Voyage to the Houyhnhnms," *Journal of English Literary History,* XVIII (1951), 275.

negative and despairing conclusion; yet Swift himself denied that he intended such an effect, and it is foreign to the nature of great art. Most important of all, if man is apart from the rest of creation, what *is* his nature? Does *Gulliver* indicate only what he is *not*?

We can, I believe, clarify these matters if we consider the relation of Swift's theological views to his satire, bringing together the two sides of the man which tradition has separated: Jonathan Swift, satirist, and Dr. Swift the Dean. In that separation lies the principal explanation for some of the most serious misunderstandings of Swift's work.

Henry More's *Divine Dialogues* may give us a clue to Swift's method and purpose in the fourth voyage. In this dialogue the different speakers represent points of view which were conflicting for supremacy. One of the most urgent problems had been raised by the theory of the plurality of worlds. What about the salvation of rational beings who may well exist in distant planets—as well as in remote places of our own earth? It is suggested that they may be creatures, endowed with reason, who have never experienced the fall. Such beings would have no need of "that Religion that the sons of *Adam* are saved by." They would live a perfectly orderly but monotonous existence, and "no Properties but those either of the *Animal* or *middle* life" would be needed. "In virtue whereof they may be good *Naturalists,* good *Politicians,* good *Geometricians* and Analysts, good *Architects,* build Cities and frame Commonwealths, and rule over their *brother*-Brutes in those Planets, and make as good use of them as we doe. . . . " [2] But this is nothing but a "middle" life, for all its placid excellence. The heights of human existence, the glory of knowing God, as well as (by implication) the depths, are outside their ken.

These creatures remind us of the Houyhnhnms, who also are good politicians, mathematicians, etc., and lead the perfect "middle" life. Swift's ultimate point in his satire is to be produced through development of a situation in which a well-meaning but not enlightened man is thrown among such rational beings, and finds that they have as servants "brother-Brutes" representing those very qualities which the fall has produced in human nature, carried to the extreme. The dilemma and despair of that man, in his inevitable failure to be able to emulate the patterns of perfection, in his failure

---

[2] *Divine Dialogues, containing Sundry Disquisitions & Instructions concerning the Attributes and Providence of God* (London, 1668), 529.

to understand the whole situation, would be those of anyone who attempts to account for human nature without original sin.

Swift many times asserted his faith in the traditional Christian view of man as interpreted by conservative Anglicanism. In his satirical version of Collins's *Discourse of Free-Thinking* (1713) he asserted that the doctrine of original sin is "the foundation of the whole Christian religion; for if men are not liable to be damned for Adam's sin, the Christian religion is an imposture." [3] A little farther on he declares: "So I affirm original sin, and that men are now liable to be damned for Adam's sin, to be the foundation of the whole Christian religion"; but, he observes, the whole doctrine now is disputed by divines and any freethinker therefore may deny the whole Christian faith.

Nor was Swift merely an official public apologist for the church which furnished his profession. In his personal statement of belief, *Further Thoughts on Religion,* he wrote that

> the Scripture system of man's creation is what Christians are bound to believe, and seems most agreeable of all others to probability and reason. . . . After his eating the forbidden fruit, the course of nature was changed, the animals began to reject his government; some were able to escape by flight, and others were too fierce to be attacked. . . . Lions, bears, elephants, and some other animals are strong or valiant, and their species never degenerates in their native soil, except they happen to be enslaved or destroyed by human fraud: But men degenerate every day, merely by the folly, the perverseness, the avarice, the tyranny, the pride, the treachery, or inhumanity of their own kind.

The fall, then, is an actual event, which produced actual, hereditary changes. In "An Evening Prayer," Swift refers repeatedly to our "corrupt nature" and to our need for divine grace. The sermon "On the Testimony of Conscience" refutes the proposition that men's natural faculties are sufficient moral guides.

What specifically was this doctrine of original sin? Swift had only

[3] *Swift's Writings on Religion and the Church,* ed. Temple Scott (London, 1898), I, 177. All citations from Swift's religious works are from this edition; those from *Gulliver* are quoted from the edition of Arthur E. Case (New York, 1938). I should add that I do not claim More as a "source," although Swift was interested in More's ideas, and had his works in his library. Rather, More serves as a valuable indication of what was in the air.

contempt for clergymen who neglected the Thirty-nine Articles, and we may without much doubt take these formulations as expressing Swift's own beliefs. Article IX, "Of Original or Birth Sin," is worth quoting at some length:

> Original sin standeth not in the following of Adam (as the Pelagians do vainly talk), but it is the fault and corruption of the nature of every man, that naturally is engendered of the offspring of Adam whereby man is very far gone from original righteousness, and is of his own nature inclined to evil, so that the flesh lusteth always contrary to the spirit, and therefore in every person born into this world, it deserveth God's wrath and damnation. And this infection of nature doth remain, yea in them that are regenerated, whereby the lust of the flesh, . . . which some do expound the wisdom, some sensuality, some the affection, some the desire of the flesh, is not subject to the law of God. And although there is no condemnation for them that believe and are baptized: yet the apostle doth confess that concupiscence and lust hath of itself the nature of sin.

The Article rejects the extreme of total depravity and implies the existence of free will; but it assumes that original sin is more than a mere "privation" or defect of original reason and righteousness. While man has the rational faculty, he yet has a positive tendency to do evil, a mysterious dynamic spirit of perversity for which there is explanation in Genesis and remedy in the Gospel. The Article, moreover, roundly condemns the "vain talk" of the Pelagians. Their position—which, as we shall see, had special importance in Swift's time—was that human nature is the same now as in the beginning, that corruptions are those of society rather than of the soul, and that the good and even perfect life is always possible if men will only do their best.

It follows that man's position is unique. There is something of the Yahoo even in the best, for the complete transformation of human nature is a miracle the Scripture leads us to expect only at the culmination of history. For a unique problem a unique solution is provided. Thus the situation of humanity is not that described, for example, in Pope's *Essay on Man*—"this isthmus of a middle state"; man is not simply a link, so to speak, joining the lower and upper worlds. This Platonizing idea, characteristic of Renaissance humanism, would in fact take away all significance of the fall as an event which made humanity *sui generis,* and not merely a part fitting into the great mosaic of a patterned universe. Swift's vehement insistence on the reality of the fall takes on its significance against this background.

Gulliver was written in an age when new beliefs were abroad and long-buried heresies were rising up in new forms. Swift especially detested the deists, with their reliance on reason. And there had originated, before Swift wrote *Gulliver,* the potent concept of the innate "moral sense." According to this theory as formulated by Shaftesbury, the human being is naturally adapted to live virtuously in the universe, and if he fails to do so it is because his training and man-made environment somehow warp the instinctive operation of the sense of right and wrong. This was a revival, on a secular level, of that Pelagianism which the church opposed. The question of human nature was involved also in the rising faith of "progress," which assumed a perfecting of human behavior in proportion to the increase of knowledge. All of these ideas, with their emphasis on men's completeness and self-sufficiency, would have seemed to Donne no less than to Swift signs of an "age of pride." The peculiar passion with which Swift attacked that vicious propensity to pride in man is understandable.

Swift's famous letter of September 29, 1725, to Pope makes it clear that *Gulliver* is to present the truth about human nature in opposition to illusion. When he says that man is incorrectly defined as "animal rationale," but is really "rationis capax," he suggests that reason works against powerful counter-tendencies and can succeed only with effort. When he says that "the whole building of my travels is erected upon this great foundation of misanthropy (though not in Timon's manner)" he makes a remark perfectly in keeping with the Christian tradition. For the doctors of the church never hesitated to point out that human nature with its tendency toward sin is hateful, and the spectacle of life, viewed in one dimension, is not one to encourage love for the species. But human nature exists in another dimension as well, for there are those who through divine mercy rise above the limitations of the race. So "all my love is toward individuals," Swift confesses.

The doctrine of the fall of man explains much of the mystery of the Houyhnhnms, and of Gulliver's relation to them. It seems to be a mistake to say that Gulliver is somewhere between the Yahoos and the rational horses. The fact of original sin makes the relationship much more subtle and elusive than that. The Yahoos are the hypostatization of those irrational, wild drives toward evil which men inherit. The tradition of the origin of the Yahoos, we hear in the ninth chapter, is that "two of these brutes appeared together upon a mountain." These first two, it was said, "had been driven thither over the sea," and had by degrees degenerated; and these "creatures could not be *ylnhiamshy* (or aborigines of the land) because of the violent hatred the Houyhnhnms, as well as all other animals, bore them." The parallel of this account with that of the change of men after the fall, as given in the *Further Thoughts,* is striking. The point of the insistence that the Yahoos are not aborigines lies in the fact that the present nature of man, with its dynamic "concupiscence and lust," does not belong to the regular order of the original creation. This fact helps explain Swift's use of the tradition of the "happy beast." The point is not that men should emulate the animals, even though the latter possess a constancy and integrity of nature which contrast with men's tendency to degeneration; for the plan of redemption raises man potentially to a glory animals can never know. But potentially only; and if the possibility is great, so is the danger of degradation.

The evidences of the depravity of our nature as revealed by the conduct of the Yahoos are too familiar to need repetition at length. Most significant is the fact that the concupiscence of these creatures is without purpose and inexplicable in terms of any truly utilitarian desires. The Yahoos' behavior is not merely a manifestation of the impulse to survive: their actions are unique in their utter lack of point. Thus the Yahoos are "violently fond of certain shining stones of several colours," which they hoard. "My master said, he could never discover the reason of this unnatural appetite, or how these stones could be of any use to a Yahoo." How indeed can a rational animal—rational "naturally"—understand the "sons of Adam"? The Houyhnhnm master never really comprehends the Yahoo society as Gulliver describes it to him, in contrast with the patriot king of Brobdingnag, who despite his own exemplary virtue, understands English behavior perfectly. But the king of Brobdingnag shares human characteristics and so can enter into the minds of human beings as the Houyhnhnm cannot.

Again, Gulliver observes that "friendship and benevolence are the two principal virtues among the Houyhnhnms, and these not confined to particular objects, but universal to the whole race. . . . They will have it that Nature teaches them to love the whole species, and it is reason only that maketh a distinction of persons, where there is a superior degree of virtue." Now friendship and benevolence were favorite words with Shaftesbury and his school, who sought to show that if men would only follow their real "nature" they would exemplify these qualities. In *Considerations upon Two Bills,* a few years after *Gulliver,* Swift wrote: "There are no qualities more incident to the frailty and corruption of human kind than an indifference, or insensibility for other men's sufferings, and a sudden forgetfulness of their own former humble state, when they rise in the world." So the irony of *Gulliver* arises in part from the fact that it is only in beings of another species that "nature" can *guarantee* friendship and benevolence. Not that men never show friendship and benevolence; but they do not act from these motives without thought and the assistance of grace.

But there may also be some hints that, as More speculated, fallen man may attain a height which unfallen beings cannot reach. The friendship and benevolence of the Houyhnhnms, so rational and so cold, are very different from the pity and love which, for example, the "little" Glumdalclitch shows for Gulliver among the Brobdingnagians. It is difficult to believe that Swift, who showed such strong attachment in his friendships, could seriously have expected us to admire the complete lack of affection in a human sense among the Houyhnhnms. The grief of Gulliver for his master contrasts strongly with the cool benevolence of the latter, as in the following passage, which with great skill projects an emotional atmosphere of the repellent around a theoretically admirable virtue.

> When all was ready, and the day came for my departure, I took leave of my master and lady, and the whole family, my eyes flowing with tears, and my heart sunk with grief. But his Honour, out of curiosity, and perhaps (if I may speak it without vanity) partly out of kindness, was determined to see me in my canoe, and got several of his neighbouring friends to accompany him.

After all, Christianity teaches that it was love and compassion in the divine that made possible the redemption of the human family. And in consequence the redemption of the sons of Adam may produce a moral grandeur which the purely rational can never know.[4]

_____
[4] The Houyhnhnms, with their complete *apatheia* and their separation of benevolence from emotion, perfectly exemplify qualities of the Stoics. This fact

Overemphasis on the "misanthropy" of the fourth voyage indeed has until recent years tended to obscure the positive element in the satire. Gulliver himself proves that men can behave with dignity and goodwill. When he leaves this utopia, he first encounters savages, who shoot arrows at him; he is rescued and treated kindly by European sailors—suggesting that the notion of virtue being primitive and instinctive, but thwarted by civilization, is wrong. *Gulliver* teaches that society, despite its many possibilities of evil, is one of the means of salvation. The Brobdingnagian state shows, not perfection, but the kind of relative goodness which is available to humanity. Under a virtuous and wise king this state has attained stability and an environment which enables men to develop in freedom. Its patriot king, no benevolent despot, establishes conditions which make possible human development. Perhaps the greatest element of hope lies in the fact that the kingdom has been regenerated from an earlier state of civil conflict between the three estates. A succession of three good rulers has brought its institutions back to their original vigor. A good constitution thus remains one of the means which men can use to free themselves in part from the limitations of their natures. By implication, too, we see that there is no inevitable drift in history. Each generation, with the assistance of the means provided to alleviate man's estate, makes its estate. Swift sternly opposed any fanatical belief that some great revolution would produce an unending world of happiness and harmony; but men are never beyond redemption, either.

The close of *Gulliver's Travels* is a comedy of irony which grows very naturally out of the confusion of fallen with unfallen natures Gulliver, carried away by the idea that men should be like the

may point to the revival of Stoicism, which many eighteenth-century writers satirized. It may also be in point here that Swift in his sermons declares that the pagan philosophers, however exalted in ideals, are never adequate guides to the good life, since they lack the knowledge which revelation provides. He was very positive about this. To regard Swift as a classical moralist with only a tincture of Christianity is out of keeping with the whole tenor of his work. For more evidence, I refer to an article of mine, "Swift and the World-Makers," in *Journal of the History of Ideas*, Jan., 1950. Bolingbroke, in a letter of 1731 to Swift, boasts ". . . that I have ventured to start a thought which must . . . render all your metaphysical theology both ridiculous and abominable." Here is a recognition of Swift's allegiance to "theology"; and Bolingbroke, despite Swift's high opinion of him, is on this matter assuredly one of "vous autres" to whom Swift refers in the letter quoted below.

Houyhnhnms, falls into despair and an absurd infatuation for an impossible ideal. In his preoccupation with the unattainable ideal he cannot see the possible one. Swift, in the letter of November 26, 1725, to Pope, confided, "I do not hate mankind." It is only, he said, "vous autres" who would have them "reasonable animals" and who are angry for being disappointed, who really hate them. That is, realism about human nature, recognizing its limitations and its real potentialities, is not truly pessimistic. Only those who expect the impossible fall into misanthropy. In this statement Swift seems to foresee what the exaggerated optimism of the age of pride would produce—the Romantic irony of the Byronic generation.

In the light of Christian doctrine we can understand the subtle relationship of the Yahoo to the civilized man—a point on which Gulliver falls into great confusion. The truth is that the man of goodwill is both redeemed and a son of Adam. Article IX warns us that "this infection of nature doth remain, yea in them that are re-generated, whereby the lust of the flesh, . . . is not subject to the law of God." In terms of Swift's symbolism, the best of men can never entirely transcend the Yahoo nature, and pride can reach no higher point than to fancy that anyone has done so. Yet regeneration is a fact, too; and in this paradox lies the secret of revelation, which mere observation, however acute, can never discover. We see, then, that there can be no true "satiric norm," no pattern of human perfection against which defects are set. Nor is there any permanent pattern of perfection among civilizations. The culminating irony of *Gulliver* is that when we finally arrive in a utopia, we find it is the land of another species.

Professor Ricardo Quintana has observed that "the softening of ethical doctrine and the rise of sentimentalism induced a certain amount of that horror which critics began to feel for *Gulliver's Travels,* particularly part IV." [5] True enough; but something more than a general "softening of ethical doctrine" was involved. The abandonment of the whole great Christian tradition was the issue. *Gulliver* is not, however, like most defenses of religion in the time, a polemic. It is something far more effective, a supreme artistic image of human life in several societies, so constructed as to bring out the true characteristics of the human being and thus indirectly

[5] *The Mind and Art of Jonathan Swift* (New York, 1936), 294.

expose the fallaciousness of illusory ideas. These ideas, not man himself, are the object of the satire. At the end we reach the limits of the human, being left with the bankruptcy of the "natural" man, and are forced to seek guidance from beyond our own resources.

That Swift the divine and Swift the artist are one and the same as to opinions is shown by the uncompromising way in which the satirist uses the old-fashioned theological terms, such as "the degenerate nature of man." But we must remember that this is satire, and hence emphasizes the negative, what is *not* true and good. To see the positive, the matrix of faith in which *Gulliver* is set, we must go to the Christian moralist. By so doing we can place men, Yahoos, and Houyhnhnms in proper perspective. And only by understanding Swift the Dean can we lay the ghost of Swift the misanthrope.

Gulliver's Travels

by Maynard Mack

That Swift's greatest satire, *Gulliver's Travels,* is sometimes elegated to the nursery can be explained in part by the fact that most adults are unwilling to face the truth about themselves.

Gulliver, who is Swift's *persona* in this work, is more complex and more complexly used than the assumed identities we have met in the *Argument* and the *Modest Proposal.* He is, first of all, a stolid, unemotional, but candid and reliable observer. In this respect, his account has been made to resemble those of the authentic voyagers of Swift's time, whose narratives of distant lands (it was the last great age of exploration) were devoured by Augustan readers. Voyages, both authentic and imaginary, were in fact one of the prominent literary genres. The intent of the imaginary voyages was almost always to satirize the existing European order, and it did so by playing up the innocence, manliness, and high ethical standards of the untutored peoples whom the voyager claimed to have met. But the real voyages also, even those recounted by missionaries and priests, pointed to the same conclusion. Reflecting, without realizing it, the general modern rehabilitation of "nature" (in contrast to the older view of nature as fallen and in need of redemption), all these voyages tended alike to stress the goodness of unspoiled primitive man. The human nature presented in such accounts (and in a substantial tradition of other writings ranging from Montaigne to Rousseau) did not appear to be morally unreliable, or controllable only by the disciplines of civilization. On the contrary, it was evidently instinctively good, and had been corrupted by civilization;

"Gulliver's Travels." From the Introduction to *English Masterpieces*, V, *The Augustans*, 2nd, ed. Maynard Mack, pp. 14-16. Copyright © 1961 by Prentice-Hall, Inc. Reprinted by permission of Prentice-Hall, Inc.

if these corrupting influences could be removed, there was practically
no limit to its perfectibility.

Swift, whose aim in *Gulliver* is (among other things) to show the
fatuity of this creed, deliberately adopts the voyage genre of the
enemy and turns it to his own ends. Wherever Gulliver goes among
his fantastic aborigines, he is always encountering, instead of handsome and noble savages, aspects of man as he perennially is, whether
in civilized society or in nature. Among the Lilliputians, it is human
pettiness, especially moral pettiness, and the triviality of many of
the forms, titles, customs, pretenses, and "points of honour" by
which men assert their dignity and about which they conduct their
quarrels. Characteristically, the devices Gulliver meets with in this
country are those of little men: pomposity, intrigue, and malice.
Among the Brobdingnagians, on the other hand, it is the physical
grossness of the human species, its callous indifference to what it
flings aside or tramples underfoot: "For I apprehended every moment that he would dash me against the ground, as we usually do
any hateful little animal which we have in mind to destroy." In this
country, Gulliver is constantly being appalled by circumstances of
coarseness: the nurse's monstrous breast, the linen "coarser than
sackcloth," the Queen crunching "the wing of a lark, bones and all,
between her teeth," and drinking "above a hogshead at a draught"
—or else of callused contempt: the schoolboy's hazelnut, the farm-
er's indifference to Gulliver's fatigue, the pet lamb promised to
Glumdalclitch but casually dispatched to the butcher. At the same
time (for in this voyage the satire cuts two ways), Gulliver's conversa-
tions with the King throw a frightful light on man as civilized
European.

The fourth voyage brings us the Yahoos and the animal nastiness
that is also one aspect of the human situation. The Yahoos are
Swift's climactic answer to the contemporary infatuation with noble
"natural" men; and the language used of them becomes especially
vulgar and anatomical to indicate the repulsiveness of "unspoiled"
nature, either physical or moral. But the Yahoos are also something
more. We may see embodied in them that extreme view of man as
hopelessly irrational, decadent, and depraved, which extreme Puri-
tanism fostered in religious terms, and which had been exemplified
in nonreligious terms by Hobbes's portrait of life in a state of nature
as "nasty, brutish, and short." This view, it will be observed, Swift
embodies in the Yahoos only to reject it. Though Gulliver makes

the error of identifying himself and other human beings completely with the Yahoos, we and Swift do not. Nor do we take the ideal life for man, as Gulliver does, to be the tepid rationality of the horses. Reacting against the Yahoos because he mistakes the animal part of human nature which they represent for the whole, Gulliver goes to the other extreme and worships pure rationality in the Houyhnhnms, which is likewise only a part of the whole. Neither extreme answers to the actual human situation, and Swift, despite the persistence with which this voyage has been misinterpreted, is careful to show us this. That Gulliver's self-identification with the Yahoos is mistaken, we realize (if we have not realized it long before) as soon as we see Gulliver insisting that his wife and children are Yahoos, and preferring to live in the stable. Similarly, we see the mistakenness of his desire to be like the Houyhnhnms as soon as we pause to reflect that they are horses: Swift has used *animals* as his symbols here in order to make it quite plain that pure rationality is not available to *man*—would make us as absurd, monstrous, and tedious as the Houyhnhnms. For the truth, as we are meant to realize, is that man is neither irrational physicality like the Yahoos nor passionless rationality like the Houyhnhnms; neither (to paraphrase Swift's own terms in a famous letter to Pope) *animal implume bipes* nor *animal rationale*, but *animal rationis capax*.

And now, if we look back again at the voyages, we can see that this middle view has been the theme from the very beginning. In Lilliput, the vices and trivialities of the little people are seen against the normal humanity and benevolence of Gulliver. In Brobdingnag, over against Gulliver's unconscious brutality in recommending gunpowder and the description of Europeans as "the most pernicious race of little odious vermin that nature ever suffered to crawl upon the face of the earth," Swift shows us the magnanimity of the King and the tenderness of Glumdalclitch. Even in the last and darkest voyage, we are never allowed to suppose (witness the Portuguese seacaptain) that real human beings are the detestable creatures Gulliver supposes them. Man is fallen so far as Swift is concerned, and the new notions of natural goodness and infinite perfectibility are nonsense; but man is also—to put it in the nonreligious terms that Swift has chosen for his parable—capable of regeneration: *rationis capax*.

Swift's instrument in this blending of light and shadow is the assumed identity, Gulliver. Through Gulliver, Swift is able to deliver the most powerful indictment of man's inhumanity ever writ-

ten in prose, and at the same time to distinguish his own realistic
view of man's nature from the misanthropy of which he has sometimes been accused. While Gulliver is still naïve, mainly in the first
two voyages, satire can be uttered through him, he himself remain-
ing unaware of it. Later, when he begins to fall into misanthropy,
still more corrosive satire can be uttered by him. But in the end
satire is uttered of him, and we see his mistake. For we discover, if
we look closely, that all through the fourth voyage Gulliver is represented as becoming more and more like a horse—learning to neigh,
to walk with an equine gait, to cherish the ammoniac smell. He is
represented, in other words, as isolating himself from mankind, and
it is only this isolation in its climactic form that we see in his treatment of his family and his residence in the stables at the close. To
suppose, as many careless critics have done, that Swift is recommending this as an *ideal* for man is the consequence of the fatal error
mentioned earlier—of identifying the author of an Augustan work
with its *persona*.

Conclusion to *Jonathan Swift* and the Age of Compromise

by Kathleen Williams

The late seventeenth and early eighteenth centuries constitute our great age of satire, the period when irony and obliquity seemed to many writers the most appropriate way of presenting their views on the subjects important to them, and it was appropriate because of certain conditions prevailing in the various spheres of life with which writers were concerned. Inheriting the Renaissance positives of nature and reason, the absolute standards of goodness and truth, which their predecessors had confidently celebrated, they found their positives inadequately interpreted and their beliefs assailed from all sides. In this situation a firm presentation of positive values was a hazardous undertaking, and difficult to achieve on any but a small scale. The most profound and inclusive statements of value to be found in the literature of the time are satiric: the close of *The Dunciad*, "Of the Use of Riches," "Of the Characters of Women," the fourth book of *Gulliver's Travels*. Traditional acceptances can now be best supported and expressed by attacking what is hostile to them, and by a shifting process of adjustment, compromise, balance. The single truth can be neither grasped in thought nor embodied in words; singleness and simplicity now only exist in the false abstractions of modern thinking. But a modest approximation to truth, a modest certainty, can be achieved and expressed by that strenuous and agile effort which issues in the serious Augustan wit.

Positive truth is now best presented by implication, through the deployment of negative materials.

Among the great Augustans who looked to the integral life of the past and strove to protect and to adapt what still survived against the inroads of the Enlightenment, Swift is the most indirect, most shifting, yet most inexorable, of all. He is deeply conscious of the disturbing tendencies of the age and very earnest in carrying out the task that seems so urgent to him as the moralist he always—and rightly—claimed to be and as a man whose personal need to feel himself in control of experience is peculiarly strong. His materials and their organization, the form and content of the satires, are his response to a particular situation at a time when, within man and without, chaos constantly threatened. Defense was essential, yet it could be achieved only by vigilant attack, sustained simultaneously on many fronts. Our first impression, in Swift's work, is of the elusive brilliance of the attack; a glancing, dazzling mind appears to be concerned solely with the presentation of absurdity or of evil, shifting its point of view constantly the better to perform its task. But as we grow accustomed to his ways of thinking and feeling we become aware that at the heart of Swift's work are unity and consistency, and we see that the attack is also a defense, that tools of destruction are being employed for a positive and constructive purpose. The inventiveness and resourcefulness of his satiric method are seen as arising directly out of the necessities of his mind and of his age; the changing complications of his irony are the necessary expression of an untiring devotion to the few certainties that life affords. For all his elusiveness and indirection, his readiness to compromise or to change his ground, few writers have been more essentially consistent than Swift, but for him consistency could be sustained only by such methods as these. Balance in the state or in the individual mind could be kept only by an agile shifting of weights.

Because Swift's indirections are governed always by a firm central purpose, it can be particularly misleading in his case to isolate one example or one aspect of his work. Letters, sermons, poems, sets of stray "Thoughts," political pamphlets, are all governed by the same attitudes and the same basic beliefs; technical satiric devices are never arbitrarily chosen, simply as the most devastating weapons available, but perform a more positive task and so are never merely attack. The stock terms in which simpler satires can be criticized are of little use for Swift. In him, parody of the style of a period or of a writer becomes a moral comment on mental habits and on wrong beliefs; a "device" which may serve a lesser writer for satiric distance and force must present in itself Swift's vision of those deeper ills in man which underlie our particular failings. That the device of relative size, in Books I and II of *Gulliver's Travels*, enables man to be seen from a startling angle is the least of its effects, for the relation of giant, pygmy, and man contributes not only to satiric attack but to the presentation of humanity and its predicament. Through relativity we are shown man's insecurity and insignificance, his dependence on physical circumstance. The Lilliputians in their fragility perfectly display the temptations of man as a political animal, efficiently but ruthlessly organized for his own defense and too ready to see morality in terms of the state; the Brobdingnagians show us the goodness of man who sees the state in terms of morality, and whose energies are devoted to the simplest and truest of human values. These figures do more than attack; they are symbols, as much embodiments of individual insight as are the images of a poet, and the same is true of the Yahoos and Houyhnhnms and the terrible immortals of Luggnagg. Behind them all is a constant view of life in which intellectual conviction and personal necessity coincide; passion as well as thought has contributed to Swift's power of imaginative realization.

Since method in Swift arises from the center of his deeply and sometimes desperately held convictions, the more fully we explore those convictions, becoming familiar with them from his writings both public and private, the more deeply we can respond to the great satires themselves. For what we see in *Gulliver's Travels* is the culmination of a long process visible everywhere in Swift, a process of investigation, of moving tentatively among conflicting opinions, testing and trying them against that central conviction which in his satiric writing can be only unobtrusively present. The task that faced him is most clearly to be seen, perhaps, in the early odes, where unattainable order and inescapable chaos are sharply and despairingly opposed, where images of confusion and deceit proliferate to overwhelm the steady light of truth. And in the poems too can be seen Swift's response to the situation which the odes present. Abandoning the attempt to find and to express the single, simple truth, he accepts a less heroic but more painstaking role and plunges into giddy circumstance, working to achieve in the confusion of the world of sense a less ambitious order. When he resolves to end, "with a puff," the delusion of exalted poetry he resolves also to explore the world of sublunary nature, source of all delusions, and to content himself with those fragments of truth which may with difficulty be related to one another. For though perfection is indeed beyond the Empyreum, and reserved for glory, yet there is a "discreet modest aequipoize of Judgment, that becomes the sons of Adam."

For Swift as much as for Sidney or Milton, true order is moral order, and any "system" which has no relation to moral good and evil is to him a danger. Most dangerous of all are those which falsely claim to have found the single truth, and so appeal in their clarity and simplicity to men weary of the difficulties of their human state and seeking a way of escape. All such schemes, in every sphere, ignore some aspect of reality and so are doomed to failure; no system whether of politics or morality or philosophy can succeed if it fails to reckon with the facts of human nature and human experience, for success to Swift means not theoretic consistency, however intellectually satisfying, but practical moral results. It is this preoccupation which leads him to emphasize so strongly the importance of experience as the basis for all human endeavor. That we should keep close to experience—our own experience gained, as Locke would have had it, from the senses and from reflection, and the ordered experience of the past which is traditional wisdom—this is the first step toward reasonable living, for though experience can delude, it is our only basis for reaching such certainty as we can. Christian doctrine as presented by his own church is important to Swift primarily as a "scheme" which, once revealed, can stand the test of experience and indeed is the only way of making sense of our world without omission, since human reason is so involved with our passions and prejudices that our attempts to free it can only lead to a more complete delusion. His attitude to all theoretical constructs of the human mind is a skeptical one, for he sees them, not as honestly ordering experience but as dishonestly ignoring it. Romanticism, sentimental patriotism, reliance on "inner light" or on reason alone, are all delusive because all depend upon a password, a simple magical formula unrelated to the conditions of life. Swift's anti-romantic poems are, like Johnson's later strictures on classical and pre-romantic poeticizing, attacks on a very real danger of the time, the tendency to substitute for hard realistic thinking and feeling a ready-made theory, whether of literature or of conduct.

Swift's dealings with political matters show clearly these central concerns. The state, like everything else, must be set in relation to moral standards before it can be seen in proportion and properly evaluated, but since it has its origins in human needs it must be seen also as part of the muddled life of man. There is no simple answer to political problems, for the state has grown through trial and error, through the pressure of experience, and it is not a planned and consistent thing. To try to impose consistency upon it, cutting through those growths which have developed through necessary adjustment to the vagaries of life, would be dangerous. It would also be a waste of time; for men of Swift's generation the reorganized state of the Commonwealth, which so quickly crumbled under the pressure of chaotic circumstance, was still a vivid lesson. A country may be organized according to the best and most reasonable theory, as the Venetian state had been, but in the end it must stand or fall by the people who compose it, and what is theoretically perfect is not likely to work well in practice, since clarity is usually achieved only by evading some of the facts. Swift will go no further toward a theory of government than to suggest that the Gothic system works best in England—a suggestion which is itself based on a consideration of the country's past experience—and the Gothic system is the most flexible of all, since it depends on the sensitive interrelation of the three sources of power. The modern state has developed in the way that events and persons compelled it, and in doing so it has not followed moral and Christian principles, so that its schemes of wealth and power are, in the last analysis, wrong. But the task of the good man in the modern commercial state is not the easy negative one of condemnation; he can still behave morally and charitably and try to persuade governments to undertake the positive encouragement of virtue. The state can never be a perfect embodiment of moral truth, but it can and should be constantly aware that within the limits laid down by human weakness it can contribute to good. Individual corruption can wreck the best theory of government, but equally virtue in individuals, both governing and governed, can produce moral and physical well-being, provided that the state is seen for what it is, a collection not of economic units nor of disinterested rational beings, but of fallible men and women, to deal with whose passions and prejudices continual flexibility, adjustment, and compromise are essential.

Thus in the political sphere is visible Swift's characteristic approach to the problems of human activity. He does not lôse sight of his central principles, but he finds that in practice these principles are best sustained through adaptability, for they can never be fruitfully considered except in relation to "John, Peter, Thomas, and so forth," to the way human beings really act, think, and feel. The actuality against which all systems must finally strike is that of human nature, and, set against one another, theories and individuals present only the barren opposition of the early poems, that between unreal order and real confusion. The only remedy is to build a tentative and approximate order from confusion itself, one which will allow for human oddity. This is always Swift's compromise solution, the only way in which something like moral order can be attained, for man, being incalculable, will break out of any system and can only be accounted for by the most flexible, inclusive, and empirical of methods. The conception of man as a creature ruled by self-love was the most adaptable of contemporary approaches to a definition, for it allows for degrees of goodness and, handled as Swift handles it, can form a basis for improvement without departing from a realistic interpretation of human possibilities. It can be reconciled not only with Swift's experience of individual men but with Christian tradition, and so is a firmer basis for morality than those schemes which, in striving to avoid sin by an appeal to the dignity of human nature, fall into the greatest sin of all, the pride which is displayed, at the end of his story, by Lemuel Gulliver. Like so many of Swift's inventions, the philosophers and Aeolists of *A Tale of a Tub*, the Laputians and the sorry heroes of the anti-romantic poems, Gulliver in trying to avoid the deceiving senses and passions has fallen further into matter. Swift's fear and hatred of the mindless, the merely material, is everywhere apparent, but if surrender to matter is evil so is the attempt to escape from it by whatever means. Both attitudes must end in deceit and death, for both deny the uniqueness of man, the "mingled Mass of Good and Bad" whose function is to wrest meaning and goodness from the chaotic "matter" of his own nature and of the world he lives in. Nothing could be further from the truth than to see Swift as a destructive and negative satirist; his purpose in destroying false and unrealistic simplifications is to show us the only conditions upon which life can be fully and creatively lived. As he himself claims in his letters to Pope, his is a constructive approach to his fellow man, in the long run kinder and more helpful than the optimistic enthusiasm of those who expect him to be not *animal rationis capax* but *animal rationale,* interpreting the ancient definition to imply that man can be summed up in terms of reason as a beast is summed up in terms of instinct. For in fact much of the goodness man is capable of arises not from reason but from feeling, if that feeling is guided by a reason and a conscience subject to religion. Swift never believed that rational benevolence or action for the good of the species was possible for fallen humanity; in Shaftesbury's terms he is, he admits by implication, a "compleat Timon or man-hater": "principally I hate and detest that animal called man." But he did believe we are capable of something that he considered to be a sounder basis for goodness; he believed in tolerance, compassion, responsiveness to one another's individual needs. His examples of such goodness are necessarily, in the terms of his satire, unobtrusive and quiet, since they represent all that is left after the destruction of mistaken aims and unrealizable ambitions, the humble endeavors of men content with the common forms, with unrefined reason and traditional wisdom, who recognize that a radical removal of prejudice may end in the loss of all that makes us human. But for all their unobtrusiveness they can be recognized as embodiments of a consistent and positive view, from the wise bee and the wise ancients and the modest sensible Martin to the giant and human figures of the *Travels,* so attractive in their touching concern for the increasingly graceless Gulliver. In *The Battle of the Books* Swift's ordering of chaos is made on the limited scale which is all he can, so far, honestly achieve; he moves among the comparative simplicities of literary and scientific argument. In *A Tale of a Tub* the emphasis is on the "uncreating word," on the sterility and inhumanity of all philosophic or religious movements which turn away from the center, from sense and experience interpreted by a humble reason. The *Tale* is Swift's own modern cobweb, fastened precariously to reality at one point only, at the figure of Martin, and through it he explores the dilemma of the odes. This is the fairyland of dreams and deceit, where for all the busy spinning of Peter and Jack, the Author and his philosophers, "the animating mind is fled," and with it moral standards; as in *The Dunciad,* "unawares Morality expires."

If this were Swift's last word his message would be incomplete, his work unsatisfying in the last resort for all its brilliance, for though his solution is present here it is lacking in force and inevitability, and it is felt as a conditional acceptance, a hypothesis rather than a conviction. But in *Gulliver's Travels* conviction is reached after a long testing of the hypothesis against experience, and is given complete expression. The madness of *A Tale of a Tub*, which is the madness of all of us, is set into place, seen in due proportion by a mature and tolerant mind. In three books human absurdities and failings are shown, but so, in Brobdingnag, are human possibilities, and in the voyage of Houyhnhnm-land the kind of moral order possible and desirable for man is more precisely displayed. Two extremes, two false simplifications, are set into relation, and the contrast between clarity and confusion is at last resolved. Between the opposed half-truths of Houyhnhnm and Yahoo, of mind and matter, stand Swift's examples of fulfilled humanity, embodying an order reached not by omission but by acceptance of complexity. The full meaning of this last book is not in any one figure but in the interrelation of them all, and its form is a perfect expression of the process of balance and inclusion by which Swift's solution is attained. Here he is successfully at grips with that problem which underlies the difficulties of politics and philosophy, science and morality, the problem of man himself, and in solving it he has produced one of the greatest, sanest, and wisest of the serious comedies of the age of compromise.

The Meaning of Gulliver's
Last Voyage

by Irvin Ehrenpreis

I

If a man consistently lies to those who have reason to trust him, he is a bad man.[1] We may soften this judgment in the face of mitigating evidence—that he is two years old, that he is a paranoid schizophrenic, and so forth; but if he is otherwise normal, such mendacity marks him as wicked. At the same time, however, we do not conceive of the normal man as wicked: a true man, "a real man,"

"The Meaning of Gulliver's Last Voyage," by Irvin Ehrenpreis. From *A Review of English Literature*, III, No. 3 (July 1962), 18-38. Reprinted by permission of the author and the British Council.

[1] In these quotations neither the italics nor the capitals of the original texts have been followed except where they have their modern significance. The account given of Part IV of *Gulliver* in this essay will be found to differ fundamentally from that given by me in earlier studies (*PMLA*, LXXII, 1957, pp. 889-95; *The Personality of Jonathan Swift*, 1958, pp. 99-109). In writing this essay, I have drawn heavily upon several sources: an unpublished lecture by Professor R. S. Crane; George Sherburn, "Errors concerning the Houyhnhnms," *Modern Philogy*, LVI, 1958, pp. 92-7; L. A. Landa, a review of my *Personality of Swift* in *Philological Quarterly*, XXXVIII, 1959, pp. 351-3; R. L. Colie, "Gulliver, the Locke-Stillingfleet Controversy, and the Nature of Man," *History of Ideas News Letter* (New York), II, 1956, pp. 58-62; O. W. Ferguson, "Swift's *Saeva Indignatio* and *A Modest Proposal*," *Philological Quarterly*, XXXVIII, 1959, pp. 473-9; Stuart Hampshire, "Criticism and Regret," in *Thought and Action*, 1959. Mr. Hampshire's phrases are sometimes echoed in my sections I and V. I am indebted to Miss Kathleen Williams of University College, Cardiff, and to Mr. Alastair Fowler of Brasenose College, Oxford, for several references used in section II. (After this article went to press, Professor Crane's lecture was published, in somewhat altered form, as "The Houyhnhnms, the Yahoos, and the History of Ideas," in *Reason and the Imagination*, ed. J. A. Mazzeo, 1962, pp. 231-53.)

is implicitly classed as good. In other words, we do think of a normal man as one who would rather speak the truth than lie. Thus, zoology apart, we carry around a definition according to which we not only distinguish but judge ourselves, and not as a sort of animal but as men.

Knowing ourselves closely, we find mitigating evidence for most of our departures from the definition; and having pardoned ourselves, we likewise and willingly excuse those we love. Indeed, the art of excusing becomes in most people so refined that they end by fencing off the original definition in order that they may act with little regard for it. The definition meanwhile remains both static and intact, always available for exhibition, though, to be sure, if the individual gladly acknowledges it, common behavior regularly insults it. Through this familiar routine, morality as a form of exploratory self-criticism is painlessly dissolved.

The problem of a moralist like Swift is less to redefine man in terms of new ideals than to knock down the fences around an accepted definition, compelling men both to measure themselves by this and to re-examine it. Now in regard to the general problem of making a definition, it is a commonplace that all classifications of concepts depend upon a single essence or a list of essential properties, and furthermore that the choice of such properties can be tested by the analysis of critical examples of the concept being defined. Thus in either choosing an essence or drawing up a list for the concept *man,* we may ask, concerning each proposed property, whether or not such and such an odd or doubtful example possesses it, or else whether or not some indubitable example lacks it. So we may wonder, Is an infant a real man? Is an idiot? An embryo? A corpse? Or we may ask, Did Socrates betray his compatriots? Did he try to preserve his children? Did he live rationally? Often we go further and manufacture unreal and even fantastic examples in order to test the criteria of *man* and thereby to separate essential from superficial qualities. If a moralist can lure people into making such tests, he can by this means force them to recognize their lack of the very properties by which they pretend to define themselves.

When the process operates the other way, from case to definition, the critical example which Swift or any moralist produces may drive an intelligent reader to make deep changes in a hitherto half-conscious conceptual scheme. Merely through being asked how his classification of human qualities would stand up in circumstances not previously envisaged—for Ugolino in the tower, or for St. Paul at the moment of conversion—a person may come to decide that powers or activities which had seemed to belong together should in fact be arranged under separate headings, that what had seemed to him divine was in fact human, and that what had seemed peculiarly a part of *man* really belonged to certain lower animals.

To such discriminations many attributes or actions which ordinarily appear human are irrelevant: an ape may wear our clothing, a bird may parrot our sounds, a dolphin may learn our games, and a young orangutang may look and act like some human babies. Yet in ordinary affairs we take the superficial token for the thing, giving to each being the benefit of his signs; for what looks like a man dressed in our clothes, speaking our words and playing our games, we start by treating as we would a real man, a normal man, a good man, even though experience and reflection may reveal him to be a criminal or a fool. And should one pursue these reflections far enough, turning them upon the unmitigated experience of one's own inexcusable conduct, one may even come—regretfully, I hope —to the paradoxical conclusion that none of the virtues essential to men are within one's particular reach. To arrive at that conclusion for any individual is still to impugn neither the separate virtues nor the definition. After all, no triangle is a perfect triangle, and the idea of health is genuine although nobody is wholly healthy. So *man* may be a valid concept though men never quite (and some men never at all) fit it; and we may therefore test its validity by applying it to borderline cases. In accordance with this line of reasoning we might as one possibility conclude that a person is human if he is in the class of creatures who both could turn into good men and try to do so.

The comical satirist differs from other moralists in that he does not argue in favor of the common definition. Rather he brings it dramatically to bear upon critical examples, startling the reader into an act of choice which he has hitherto avoided, viz. between the concept and the case. Suddenly the reader is confronted with the need either to surrender a sound definition or to strip a label from an unsound case. And this is the scheme of *A Modest Proposal*. Swift makes no attempt, in the satire, to deny the validity of the conventional idea of a normal (and therefore good) man. Rather he invokes it by implication.

As it happens, Locke had minutely examined such problems of

classification and definition when he attacked the doctrine of innate ideas. For example, in the course of his attack Locke tried to prove that no moral, or "practical," rules can be innate; and for this purpose he selected several rules which appear incontrovertibly valid, universally self-evident, or, as I should say, which appear of so fundamental an order as to identify men as human: e.g., that one should do as he would be done unto, or that men should keep their compacts, or that parents should preserve their children. Locke then proceeded to show that communities and situations existed in which each of these rules was violated:

> It is familiar among the Mingrelians, a people professing Christianity, to bury their children alive without scruple. There are places where they eat their own children. The Caribbees were wont to geld their children, on purpose to fat and eat them. And Garcilasso de la Vega tells us of a people in Peru which were wont to fat and eat the children they got on their female captives, whom they kept as concubines for that purpose, and when they were past breeding, the mothers themselves were killed too and eaten.[2]

The strength of Locke's argument depends not upon the doubtfulness of the maxim being judged but rather upon its authority. Each is a supreme law of human conduct although some people break it. "If any [moral principle] can be thought to be naturally imprinted, none, I think, can have a fairer pretence to be innate than this: 'Parents, preserve and cherish your children'" (I. ii. 12). The argument works *a fortiori:* if the most powerful, most basic moral principles can be ignored, then none can be innate.

Now we may turn Locke's implications inside out and say that when such a rule is broken, the violators mark themselves as not human. If we wish to trace the ramifications yet further, we may add that to assume that people will violate such a rule is to regard them as beasts. And this is what I believe Swift said in *A Modest Proposal.* He invoked a definition which he knew the Irish reader accepted, viz. that it is the nature of men to love their children. Next he introduced an implicit minor premise, viz. that the Irish are not to be regarded as men. Finally, he drew his conclusion, that nobody in Ireland would object to the butchering of children for the table.

[2] *Essay concerning Human Understanding,* Bk. I, chap. ii, par. 9; ed. A. C. Fraser (Oxford, 1894), I, p. 73.

The essential device in the satire is to lure the Irish reader into identifying himself with the writer. The kindly tone of the opening paragraph, the public spirit of the second, and the businesslike confidence of the third achieve this seduction. "The author and I have the same nature," says the reader—whereupon Swift replies, "You have indeed," and springs his trap. In repudiating the rest of the essay, the Irish reader must acknowledge either that his definition of man is not valid or else that his treatment of his own humble compatriots (and their indifference to such treatment) is inhuman; for three bad harvests had revealed that the sight of starving mankind affected Irish landlords as little as the sight of a slaughtered pig.[3]

II

Through the satire of *A Modest Proposal*, then, Swift takes an accepted definition of man and draws the reader into testing an example by it. The result of course should be to shock the reader into rejecting the example. Through the satire of the last part of *Gulliver's Travels*, on the other hand, Swift takes some fantastic examples of real or apparent humanity and has us test accepted definitions by them. The result this time should be to drive the reader to revise his own concepts. The object satirized is now broader, of course, than it was to become in *A Modest Proposal*; for not merely the Irish nor their landlords but rather men as such are being reproached. Similarly, the accusation presented is more general. In my terms it may be expressed as a complaint that while men talk of themselves according to one definition, they not only act according to another—which happens to conflict with the first—but ought in fact to adopt a third. To put it at first somewhat briefly, when men talk of themselves, they use the description "rational creatures." When they deal with one another, however, they rely upon superficial and external criteria such as shape and clothing. Yet the truth is that the first standard is impossible and the second is absurd. A real, normal, true man is one who tries to be rational. I should like to explore the implications of these ideas by way of an extensive diversion, mainly again through some remarks

[3] For my assumption that *A Modest Proposal* is primarily addressed to an Irish audience, see Ferguson.

of John Locke, after which I shall return to the route of Gulliver's
final voyage.

Professor Ronald S. Crane has shown convincingly that throughout this voyage Swift is playing with the maxims and illustrations
found in traditional manuals of logic. Regularly, the compilers of
these manuals define man as *animal rationale*. Among their most
common examples of *animal irrationale* is *equus*. They also employ
such sentences as *Si simia non sit irrationalis, est homo*. In distinguishing between the essential and the accidental properties of our
species, the logicians give *vestis* as *composita per accidens*. To un-
derline the importance of such data, one need only remember the
role which clothes, simians, and equines play in determining for
Gulliver the essential properties of man.[4]

Among these traditional comparisons the man-horse parallel early
became a commonplace[5] and could often therefore be invoked
ironically, in mock-logic. For instance, Sir Philip Sidney, speaking
of a friend who had been attributing high human virtues to horses,
says, "If I had not been a piece of a logician before I came to him,
I think he would have persuaded me to have wished myself a horse"
(*Defence of Poesy*, par. 2). Similarly, in *Hudibras*, Samuel Butler
says his hero would "undertake to prove by force / Of argument, a
man's no horse" (I. i. 71-2); and Hudibras, in a contrast between
synods and bears, says, "That both are *animalia*, / I grant, but not
rationalia"; Ralpho, he says, can "no more make bears of these,
/ than prove my horse is Socrates" (I. iii. 1277-8, 1281-2).

Furthermore, in serious arguments about the meaning of *individual, person,* and *species,* the two elements of the horse-man antithesis
tended to be so described as to isolate and dramatize the central
issue; for the imaginary horse is most useful in such an argument
if he is the most excellent conceivable of his kind; the imaginary
man, if he is the most degenerate. Thus the problem of defining
the human species becomes that of differentiating a rational, ideal-
ized horse from a degenerate, irrational man. Professor Rosalie L.
Colie has noticed an extreme instance of this development in the

---

[4] Cf. Narcissus, Marsh, *Institutiones logicæ* (Dublin, 1681), pp. 184-5 (*equus*),
sig. A5 (*simia*), p. 38 (*vestis*), and passim. For these important facts I am indebted
to Professor Crane, although my interpretation of them is different from his, and
the sentences about *simia* and *vestis* were not used by him.

[5] A well-known ancient example, often imitated, is the conversation between
Ulysses and the horse in the *Gryllus* dialogue of Plutarch's *Moralia*.

speculations of Anne Conway. To Lady Conway it appeared that metempsychosis and the transmutation of animal species were facts in nature. Yet she insists that such changes do not turn one essential individual into another. She can therefore make up the case of a horse which grows more excellent with each rebirth, coming nearer and nearer the nature and species of a man but retaining its essential individuality. Since, moreover, it is laid down that infinite excellence belongs only to God and Christ, the finite gap between equinity and humanity must be passable, Lady Conway says, and so must the road from man to beast; for since man, "by his voluntary transgression," has depressed his own nature into a condition as vile in spirit as the most unclean beast, "what injustice will this be, if God should also compel him to bear that image outwardly in his body, into the which he hath inwardly transformed himself?" [6] Lady Conway is trying to define a human individual so that the concept will be independent of both the rationality and the shape which are associated with the species. She chooses to start from beings who share the former while differing sharply in the latter. But the other combination—identical shape, different reasoning powers—is just as logical, and we shall find it used as well.

For Swift's generation it was a commonplace that the human body makes an insufficient mark of humanity; apes, monkeys, and monsters were invoked to prove this. Yet certain kinds of reason could also, it seemed, be found in lower animals. While, of course, the ancients were, as Swift knew, familiar with the argument that reason does not belong exclusively to mankind, it is Montaigne in particular who dramatized that argument for the tradition to which *Gulliver's Travels* belongs; and it was he above all whom Descartes intended to refute through the doctrine that animals are automatons devoid of thought. At the same time, the doctrine of animal rationality found so many simple or direct applications among the moral philosophers that some writers employed it ironically or indirectly to satirize human foolishness.[7]

[6] [Lady Anne Conway] *The Principles of the Most Ancient and Modern Philosophy* (London, 1692), pp. 71-2.

[7] See George Boas, *The Happy Beast* (Baltimore, 1933); Elizabeth Barker, "Giovanni Battista Gelli's *Circe* and Jonathan Swift," *Cesare Barbieri Courier* (Trinity College, Hartford), II, November 1959, pp. 3-15. Miss Barker's parallels between Gelli and Swift are unconvincing, but she does illuminate the traditions to which *Gulliver* belongs.

Among these is an acknowledged model for *Gulliver's Travels*, the fantastic voyages of Cyrano de Bergerac. In the moon, Cyrano finds giant men walking on all fours who mistake him for a baboon. There is a long argument as to whether or not he is an irrational animal. In Cyrano's *Histoire des oiseaux* the narrator is captured by intelligent birds. To protect himself from them, Cyrano claims to be a monkey educated and corrupted by men: "The habits and the food of these dirty beasts [i.e. men]," he says, "had acquired so much power over me that even my parents, who are monkeys of honour, would hardly recognise me now." Nevertheless, the birds argue that precisely because he is irrational, he must be a man. "Since the poor beast has not the use of reason like ourselves," says his partridge prosecutor, "I excuse his errors in so far as they are produced by lack of understanding." Cyrano is finally saved by a parrot which had belonged to a cousin and which he had often used as evidence to prove that birds can reason.[8]

Swift's master, Sir William Temple, was an admirer and imitator of Montaigne; he had read Cyrano; and he inevitably touched on the problem of animal rationality and human shape in essays which we know Swift read. In remarking that various properties have been suggested as peculiar to mankind, Temple lists the most common as reason, shape, speech, laughter, and tears. But critics of vulgar opinion, he points out, have disallowed each of these traits: e.g. the human shape has been found in "some kind of baboons, or at least such as they call drills"; and human reason, says Temple, is often attributed to such animals as dogs, owls, foxes, elephants, and horses.[9]

Even in our own day both the issue and this approach to it remain interesting, witness the following reflection by Mr. Stuart Hampshire:

If creatures from another planet, anatomically similar to men, were discovered, would we choose to call them men, if they had no language, social conventions and powers of thought and of expression above the animal level? Evidently not. If creatures from another planet, anatomically very unlike men, were discovered, would we

---

[8] Cyrano de Bergerac, *Voyages to the Sun and the Moon,* trans. Richard Aldington (London, 1923), pp. 241, 254, 260. Swift's use of Cyrano is considered in detail by W. A. Eddy, in *Gulliver's Travels: A Study in Sources* (Princeton, 1923).
[9] "Of Popular Discontents," *Miscellanea. The Third Part* (1701), pp. 1-5.

choose to call them men, if they communicated thoughts and inten-
tions in a language that we could understand? Evidently the answer
would depend on the purposes for which this classification was required. For ordinary practical purposes, and if the interests of physical science were disregarded, we would classify them as men, because
we would treat them as we treat human beings in all our ordinary
dealings with them. They would play the same, or a sufficiently
similar, part in our lives as human beings now play.[10]

III

Of all the parallels with these preoccupations of Swift the most
illuminating, I think, are those of John Locke. In the *Essay concerning Human Understanding* Locke had minutely examined the
problem of defining the human species. During the course of this
examination he made frequent use of two terms, "real essence"
and "nominal essence." For Locke the "real essence" means the
true internal constitution of particular substances or ideas; thus
whatever it is which ultimately makes a man a man, is his "real
essence." Unfortunately, however, we can never directly know the
real essence of a substance (such as man), says Locke. Instead, we
can only list the perceptible qualities by which in practice we
recognize a man, for example, as such; and the idea constituted of
these outward, observable qualities, Locke called the "nominal
essence," an abstraction. To demonstrate his lessons, Locke naturally fell back upon the traditional examples; and since he took
reason and shape to be the most important properties of the
nominal essence, he often paired off men with simians, showing
that these two properties were not necessarily tied to one another.
Here are a few of his arguments:

> There are creatures in the world that have shapes like ours, but are
> hairy, and want language and reason. There are naturals [i.e. idiots]
> amongst us that have perfectly our shape, but want reason, and some
> of them language too. There are creatures as it is said . . . that, with
> language and reason and a shape in other things agreeing with
> ours, have hairy tails; others where the males have no beards and
> the females have. If it be asked whether these be all *men* or no,
> all of human species? it is plain, the question refers only to the

[10] Hampshire, *Thought and Action,* p. 228.

nominal essence. . . . Shall the difference of hair only on the skin
be a mark of a different internal specific constitution between a change-
ling [i.e. an idiot] and a drill [i.e. a baboon], when they agree in
shape, and want a reason and speech? [III. vi. 22.]

Among the best-known passages in the *Essay concerning Human
Understanding* used to be the anecdote, anticipating Mr. Hampshire's speculation, which Locke relates to support the argument
that the word "man" as popularly, but mistakenly, employed
refers to the human shape and not to human faculties. He writes:
"Whoever should see a creature of his own shape or make, though
it had no more reason all its life than a cat or a parrot, would call
him still a *man*; or whoever should hear a cat or a parrot discourse,
reason, and philosophise, would call or think it nothing but a
cat or a *parrot*; and say, the one was a dull irrational man, and
the other a very intelligent rational parrot." He then tells the
anecdote, a supposedly true story of a parrot which could converse
like a man. Next, Locke asks whether if this parrot and all of
its race had always talked so, they would not have been treated as
rational animals, yet whether, for all that, they would not still have
been classed not as men but as parrots. "For I presume it is not
the idea of a thinking or rational being alone that makes the
idea of a man in most people's sense: but of a body so and so
shaped, joined to it" (II. xxvii. 9-10). One scholar has said that
the parrot anecdote must have left a deep impression on everyone
who read Locke's *Essay,* and that "more than one of his professed
admirers seemed to recollect little else which they had learned
from that work than the story of this parrot" (II. xxvii. 9, n. 2).
To Swift the story would have been peculiarly familiar, since he
wrote it: I mean literally, "wrote," because he did not compose it.
Locke found the anecdote in Temple's *Memoirs,* and it was Swift
who made the copy of the *Memoirs* which was sent to the printer.[11]

As early as *A Tale of a Tub* this question of accident *versus*
essence, shape *versus* reason, may have touched Swift. That such
preoccupations floated behind the clothes allegories of the *Tale*
in general and behind the outside-inside imagery of the *Digression
on Madness* in particular, is suggested by some of Locke's remarks:

[11] See Fraser's note to Locke, I, p. 446; Swift, *Correspondence,* ed. F. E. Ball
(1910-14), I, p. 172. Locke added the parrot in his 4th ed., 1700.

That all things that have the outward shape and appearance of a man must necessarily be designed to an immortal future being after this life: or, secondly, That whatever is of human birth must be so . . . is to attribute more to the outside than inside of things; and to place the excellency of a man more in the external shape of his body, than internal perfections of his soul: which is but little better than to annex the great and inestimable advantage of immortality and life everlasting . . . to the cut of his beard, or the fashion of his coat. For this or that outward mark of our bodies no more carries with it the hope of an eternal duration, than the fashion of a man's suit gives him reasonable grounds to imagine it will never wear out, or that it will make him immortal [IV. iv. 15; cf. pars. 13, 14, 16].

Although in *Gulliver's Travels* these issues are most deeply considered in the *Voyage to the Houyhnhnms,* Swift alludes to them in Brobdingnag. When the giant king first saw Gulliver, he thought the tiny man might be a piece of clockwork. "But, when he heard my voice, and found what I delivered to be regular and rational, he could not conceal his astonishment." (chap. 3) This may be an allusion to one of Descartes' arguments involving clockwork and language:

If there were machines with the organs and appearance of a monkey, or some other irrational animal, we should have no means of telling that they were not altogether of the same nature as those animals; whereas if there were machines resembling our bodies, and imitating our actions as far as is morally possible, we should still have two means of telling that, all the same, they were not real men. First, they could never use words or other constructed signs as we do to declare our thoughts to others.[12]

When the giant king asks his learned men to decide what Gulliver is, they anticipate the Houyhnhnms' attack upon the normal human form as nonviable, and they also consider whether he may be an "embrio or abortive birth" (chap. 3). This is perhaps an allusion to Locke's remark, "It has more than once been debated, whether several human foetus's should be preserved, or

[12] *Discourse on Method,* end of Pt. VI; trans. L. J. Lafleur (New York, 1950), p. 36. The argument is a recurrent one in Descartes' philosophical writings.

received to baptism, or no . . . The learned divine and lawyer, must, on such occasions, renounce his sacred definition of 'animal rationale' " (III. vi. 26).

<h1 style="text-align:center">IV</h1>

Professor R. L. Colie has supplied the next link in my chain of data: In a brilliant note which appeared six years ago, Miss Colie pointed out what is probably the intellectual background of Swift's ape-man-horse seesaw (Yahoo-Gulliver-Houyhnhnm): this is a controversy between Edward Stillingfleet and John Locke over the nature of man.[13] In the *Essay* Locke had indeed defined reason as "that faculty, whereby man is supposed to be distinguished from beasts, and wherein it is evident he much surpasses them." (IV. xvii. 1) But Locke had also directly opposed himself to Descartes; for he argued that the signs of reason do appear in lower animals. When Stillingfleet, Bishop of Worcester, wrote a defense of the doctrine of the trinity, based upon traditional logic, he said that Locke's philosophy gave comfort to anti-trinitarians; and it was from this provocation that the quarrel arose.

Stillingfleet attacked Locke's explanation of the concept of man as a "nominal essence." He followed, instead, the traditional logical formula which had been rejected by the philosopher. According to this a creature is a man through enjoying a special "subsistence" of the essence or nature peculiar to his species. Stillingfleet was blind to the problem which Locke dealt with: that since we do not directly know what the real essence of man or any other substance actually consists of, we cannot in practice use a "subsistence" of it to identify examples of humanity; and so we must rely upon perceptible qualities. Benightedly, Stillingfleet wrote: "The nature of a man is equally in Peter, James and John; and this is the common nature, with a particular subsistence, proper to each of them." It is in virtue of this fact, according to Stillingfleet, that they are distinguished by separate, proper names: "Peter, James and John are all true and real men." [14]

[13] See note 1.

[14] Quoted from Stillingfleet (*A Discourse in Vindication of the Doctrine of the Trinity*, 1697) by Locke, in his *A Letter to the . . . Bishop of Worcester* (1697), p. 195.

Locke argued that if names not obviously human were employed, the bishop would be seen to be question-begging: e.g., if Locke should ask "whether Weweena, Chuckery and Cousheda, were true and real men or no," Stillingfleet would not be able to tell. Then Locke continued:

> Body, life, and the power of reasoning, being not the real essence of a man, as I believe your lordship will agree; will your lordship say, that they are not enough to make the thing, wherein they are found, of the kind called man, and not of the kind called baboon, because the difference of these kinds is real? If this be not real enough to make the thing of one kind and not of another, I do not see how *animal rationale* can be enough really to distinguish a man from an horse.[15]

Stillingfleet answered uncomprehendingly: "Your Weweena, Cuchepy [sic] and Cousheda I have nothing to say to, they may be *drills* [i.e. baboons] for anything I know; but Peter, James and John are men of our own country." [16]

In his reply, Locke discussed the names and natures of men and drills, and brought in the horse as well:

> [Stillingfleet] says, that the nature of a man is equally in Peter, James and John. That's more than I know: Because I do not know what things Peter, James and John are. They may be drills, or horses, for ought I know . . . for I know a horse that was called Peter; and I do not know but the master of the same team might call other of his horses, James and John. Indeed, if Peter, James and John, are supposed to be the names only of men, it cannot be questioned but the nature of man is equally in them. . . . But then this to me, I confess, [seems] . . . to say no more but this, that a man is a man, and a drill is a drill, and horse is a horse.[17]

The impenetrable Stillingfleet retorted that even the owner of the horse named Peter would disagree with Locke, would be able

---

[15] *Works*, 5th ed. (1751), I, pp. 386-8 (reprinting Locke's *Letter to the . . . Bishop of Worcester*, 1697).

[16] *The Bishop of Worcester's Answer to Mr. Locke's Letter* (1697), p. 120.

[17] *Works*, I, p. 425 (reprinting *Mr. Locke's Reply to the . . . Bishop of Worcester's Answer*, 1697, pp. 132-4).

to tell the beast from a man, and would say, "My man Peter and
I can sit and chop logick together about our country affairs, and
he can write and read, and he is a very sharp fellow at a bargain;
but my horse Peter can do none of these things, and I never could
find any thing like reason in him, and do you think I do not know
the difference between a man and a beast?"[18] For fifteen (small
octavo) pages Stillingfleet continued to show how one could tell
a horse from a man and a man from a baboon (pp. 159-74).

To all this, Locke replied at greater length yet, demonstrating,
for instance, that what seem to be necessary properties of the abstract concept of man may well be lacking in specific men:

> Rationality as much a property as it is of a man, is no property of
> Peter; he was rational a good part of his life, could write and read,
> and was a sharp fellow at a bargain: But about thirty, a knock so
> altered him, that for these twenty years past, he has been able to do
> none of these things, there is to this day, not so much appearance
> of reason in him, as in his horse or monkey: and yet he is Peter
> still.[19]

That Swift would have read Locke's polemical discourses appears
probable. They were published while Swift, a studious young priest,
was living at Moor Park with Sir William Temple, often visiting
nearby London, and writing *A Tale of a Tub* and *The Battle of
the Books*. Locke's and Stillingfleet's pamphlets belonged to the
sensational trinitarian controversy which fulminated throughout
the reign of William and Mary, shook Convocation, and provoked
a royal edict. The Locke-Stillingfleet exchanges were among the
most important and notorious contributions to this warfare. Locke's
side of it was included, with the *Essay concerning Human Understanding*, in the first volume of his collected works (1714), so that
whoever looked at this form of his masterpiece would find with it
his three letters to Stillingfleet. There is little doubt that Swift
would have followed the original trinitarian controversy, or that
he read Locke's political and philosophical works. It seems likely,
therefore, that he would have met these pamphlets. Even if he

---

[18] *The Bishop of Worcester's Answer to Mr. Locke's Second Letter* (1698), pp.
160-2.

[19] *Works*, I, p. 556 (reprinting *Mr. Locke's Reply to the . . . Bishop of Worcester's Answer to His Second Letter*, 1699, p. 358).

happened to miss them, however, their themes and terms were in the air for decades.[20]

V

How does this material—supposing it to be relevant—help us to understand Gulliver's last voyage? It does seem to imply that Swift's attack is made on the broadest possible front. The object ridiculed is not Europeans, Christians, Irish landlords, or the middle class; it is mankind. From the author's point of view, all the persons in the book, apart from the Yahoos and the Houyhnhnms, are examples of the general concept *human being:* the English seamen, the Lilliputians, the Blefescudians, the Brobdingnagians, the Dutch and Japanese pirates, the Laputians; the inhabitants of Balnibarbi, Luggnagg, Glubbdubdrib, and Japan; the Dutch seamen, the English mutineers, the savage islanders, the Portuguese seamen; Glumdalclitch, the King of Brobdingnag, Lord Munodi, and Captain Pedro de Mendez. Narrower classifications—religious, national, or social groups—would not seem to be the ultimate objects, therefore, of Swift's purely moral inquiry. The human characters have no common religion, nation, or class. The group of admirable characters—the King of Brobdingnag, Lord Munodi, Captain de Mendez—are not described as more or less religious than the others. The Houyhnhnms have no revealed faith at all. One cannot, apparently, regard the Houyhnhnms or Yahoos as opposed to men in religious terms. Rather the problem seems to be to induce from the assemblage of specimens of mankind a definition which will not only comprehend them but will distinguish them from Yahoos without granting them the properties of Houyhnhnms. At the same time the effect of the varied exhibit is to disprove the validity of current definitions.

Perhaps Swift is obliging his readers to acknowledge the paradox that most of them cling to a concept of their species which

---

[20] Swift once quoted from the book by Stillingfleet which started the controversy with Locke, the *Discourse in Vindication of the Doctrine of the Trinity;* see Swift's *Prose Works,* ed. H. Davis (Oxford, 1939-), II, p. 79. Swift once owned Stillingfleet's *A Rational Account of the Grounds of the Protestant Religion* (1681); see his *Correspondence,* I, p. 28. He also owned Stillingfleet's *Origines Sacrae,* 4th ed. (1675); see Sir Harold Williams, *Dean Swift's Library* (Cambridge, 1932), item no. 334 in the sale catalogue.

would exclude their respective selves. If he is following Locke, he may be further implying that "man" as commonly used involves contradictory elements and could be split into a pair of "nominal essences," excluding the irrational from the truly human; for Locke says, "The idea of the shape, motion, and life of a man without reason, is as much a distinct idea, and makes as much a distinct sort of things from man and beast, as the idea of the shape of an ass with reason would be different from either that of man or beast, and be a species of an animal between, or distinct from both." (IV. iv. 13) Against this background the Yahoos would embody an ironical reflection upon the fact that the bulk of unthinking men do in practice treat external shape as a sounder guide to humanity than reasonable conduct. Further yet, and as the bitterest irony of all, the Yahoos seem Swift's way of showing that for practical purposes one could more easily distinguish man by his vices than by his virtues; for it is certain vices, says Gulliver, that are "rooted in the very souls of all my species" (letter to Sympson).

Contrariwise, by having the Houyhnhnms invariably act rationally, Swift defines reason so that men seem as irrational as possible. Professor Crane has shown that the common meaning of *animal rationale* was (implicitly) not an animal which in practice never diverged from reason, but one which had the power and tendency to behave rationally. By assuming that invariable rationality is the true significance of the word, Swift sharpens the satire: judged by that standard, we must all fail; and so the proper definition of man becomes limited to the class of beings like the King of Brobdingnag, who can act rationally and try to do so.

An apparent flaw in these hypotheses is that they make the Houyhnhnms out to be a positive ideal in spite of the passages where they appear absurd. To begin with, however, I do not suggest that the Houyhnhnms or any figures in the satire possess a consistent character. The voice throughout is that of Swift. He employs Gulliver and the other persons as either straightforward or ironical mouthpieces; and they have neither the independence, the consistency, nor the life of characters in a novel. Frequently, he gives them a coherent symbolic function; and he alludes to them of course as if they were people. But one cannot tell whether their actions and speeches are ironical or serious except by considering, not the relations of the characters within a narrative framework, but the implicit tone or attitudes of the author. The representation of the persons changes arbitrarily from ironical to serious as it happens to fit Swift's didactic aim.

There should be no doubt that Swift sometimes twists the Houyhnhnms' tails. One instance is the contempt thrown by Gulliver's master upon the human form divine: the flatness of our face, the prominence of our nose, etc. Not only is this attack comically hippocentric, but it recalls similar animadversions by Pliny, Plutarch, and a great train of followers.[21] Such attacks grew so frequent during the sixteenth century that Montaigne ridiculed *ces plaintes vulgaires"*;[22] and Swift, if nothing else, knew Montaigne too well to be ignorant of his arguments. Behind the Houyhnhnms' fault-finding, we can see Swift wink at us.

If, then, the Houyhnhnms represent an ideal, why does the author joke at their expense? I suppose the comprehensive answer is that Swift was a joker. Like Shaw, he often could not resist a comic opening even when the indulgence would obscure a satirical design; and so he ridicules our own anthropocentricity in the Houyhnhnms. Some comedy is inevitable, moreover, when an author tries to produce beings which share the properties of a horse at the same time as they embody the highest natural virtues. The attempt is bound to collapse on one level or the other; and the collapse is bound to seem funny.[23] The more coherence we try to impose on the Houyhnhnms, the more awkward we make Swift's procedure. Yet I think one can accept them as ideal patterns where Swift is setting them off against man's irrationality, and as comic figures where he is smiling at the whole project of bestowing concrete life upon unattainable abstractions. Finally, the jokes may be Swift's method of ridiculing platitudinous moralists who, unlike himself, pose as Houyhnhnms. He is perhaps warning the sophisticated reader that this author, unlike Gulliver, appreciates the comical aspect of his own didacticism. It need not seem odd that a tough-minded evangelist should acknowledge the quixotry of his vocational ambition: to reform the human race.

Still, that the Houyhnhnms are not in themselves pleasing to the readers of our epoch, is hardly doubtful. Supposing there were no strength in any other criticism made of Swift by Huxley, Orwell,

---

[21] See Boas, *op. cit.*, passim.
[22] *Essais*, ed. Pierre Villey (Paris, 1930), II, p. 246.
[23] Sherburn, *op. cit.*, p. 93.

and their epigones, they would remain irrefutable witnesses of
this failure. If, says Swift, we were more like the Houyhnhnms in
character, we should be better off than we are now: that is his
premise. And though his contemporaries, whether Protestant, Roman, or deist, spoke in unison with him, his readers today almost
as single-mindedly shout *No.* Here flows, between them and us,
the Styx to which I suspect Dr. Leavis was pointing when he said,
"We shall not find Swift remarkable for intelligence if we think
of Blake." [24] What indeed may mean everything to some of us—
"The road of excess leads to the palace of wisdom"—would have
meant nothing to Swift.

Nevertheless, as an element in the satire, the work of the Houyhnhnms is to represent not Swift's ideals but the reader's. It is
probable that Swift did mean to embody his own values in them;
but that is a biographical fact. Their use in the satire is to be
taken for granted, an obvious moral standard. As Professor Landa
remarks, the principles embodied in the Houyhnhnms were norma-
tive for everyone, ideals beyond definition and beyond criticism,
invoked universally to judge the faults of man.[25] But besides seeing that no moralist in Swift's own generation would have rejected his premise, we must also see that his own attitude toward
it belongs outside *Gulliver's Travels.* In the design of the book,
the Houyhnhnms stand for what we, rather than the middle-aged
Dean, consider ideal. If we could recast them to shape the view
of human possibility bequeathed to us by Blake, Kierkegaard, or
Marx, Swift's final argument would still obtain. This is perhaps
what T. S. Eliot meant when he called the conclusion of *Voyage
to the Houyhnhnms* "one of the greatest triumphs that the human
soul has ever achieved." [26]

If we proceed from Swift's line, we must still decide whether
Gulliver's behavior after conversion to the Houyhnhnms' rationality (as an ideal) is admirable or absurd. Surely, the author does not
desire us to imitate him, to secede from our families, and to live
in stables. Yet if the Houyhnhnms are admirable, one might assume that Gulliver was right to adopt what appears to be their
view of humanity. To step out of this dilemma, we may admit that

[24] "The Irony of Swift," *Scrutiny,* II, 1934, p. 378. [Reprinted in this collection.]
[25] Landa, *op. cit.,* p. 352.
[26] "Ulysses, Order, and Myth," *The Dial,* LXXV, November 1923, p. 481.

Gulliver's fate cannot be admirable in any simple sense, for it violates principles implied throughout the *Travels*—and taught by Swift in pamphlets, sermons, letters, and prayers. This step can be reconciled with the claim that the Houyhnhnms are wholly good if we decide they are not what we can directly copy, that our immediate examples live elsewhere. In judging this universal human inadequacy to be regrettable, one need not exempt Gulliver from it. He does not suppose he is free from it; for though he strives to imitate the Houyhnhnms, he never imagines he has become one. Neither does he make the opposite error of mistaking a horse's shape for the mark of a Houyhnhnm, since he laments the brutality of horses though honoring them for bearing the lineaments of his masters. It is the vision of the life of reason that nourishes his apparent misanthropy: unlike most men, Gulliver at least tries to be a "true" man; and both this attempt and the humility which it implies endow him with the ground upon which he condemns the pride of those who have less insight.

At least some of the human characters in *Gulliver* are recommended as models for men to imitate: the King of Brobdingnag, Lord Munodi, and Pedro de Mendez. It may seem a crux in interpretation that when several good people come forth to be moral examples, another ideal, in the figure of the Houyhnhnms, should be presented as well. But there can hardly be a real conflict between human and nonhuman models. Unattainable ideals are regularly set before us by moral instructors, with intermediary examples to soften our despair. In England, during Swift's lifetime, the homiletic standard of Christian perfection was, for Anglicans, not more but less strenuous than the preachments of Gulliver. The Christian, unlike the natural man, could fulfill himself in another life, and could meanwhile look for God's improving grace to support his own will. Just as, on the theological level, spirit must always be at odds with flesh, so in the moral order, conscience can never stop battling with concupiscence; and no man dare hope for the natural serenity of a Houyhnhnm.[27] We may replace the equine symbol by what ideal we please: Swift's reproach is not alone that our conduct falls short of the mark within our reach, but as well that we regard the ultimate mark as attainable. We fail to approach the Brobdingnagians, and we suppose we can be Houyhnhnms.

[27] Norman Sykes, *From Sheldon to Secker* (Cambridge, 1959), pp. 176-8.

Since Gulliver stands for any reader, his conduct after the final return to England means more than the story of an aberration. The ending of Molière's *Le Misanthrope* is another version of the same parable; for Swift may have been hinting that the influence upon Gulliver of the Houyhnhnms' ideal virtues is no more extravagant than the effects of a strict and perfect obedience to Christian ideals would be in an eighteenth century society.[28] Swift is perhaps delivering a moral analogue of the religious paradox which opens *An Argument against Abolishing Christianity*—where he says that if men did in fact practice primitive Christianity, they would destroy what they suppose to be a precious civilization. So at the close of *Gulliver's Travels*, we may suppose that he addresses himself to the latitudinarian, the sentimentalist, the Christian, the deist, and anybody else who might not only regard the character of a Houyhnhnm as admirable but also treat it as an easy ideal for humanity, and that to these he says, "If you really lived by your avowed principles, you would uproot society as Gulliver wrecks his family."

[28] Sherburn, *op. cit.*, p. 97.

A Voyage to Nowhere with
Thomas More and Jonathan Swift:
Utopia and *The Voyage to the Houyhnhnms*

by John Traugott

I. *Black and White: Henry the Beast and More the Saint*

Why did Swift, so violent a Churchman, so violently hate
Henry VIII, "founder" (so to speak, for want of a better word) of
his Church? Such apparent contradictions, which are common
enough in Swift's thought, are in fact the breath of life to the
ironist. Swift despised the trope of paradox as a species of modern
vulgarity: his "paradoxes" lead straight to the heart of his irony
—and to its absolute distinctions of value. This one will take us
to certain informing ideas of *Gulliver's Travels*.

In his pamphlet "Concerning that Universal Hatred which Pre-
vails against the Clergy," Swift the priest probes—obsessively—a
kind of original sin which he considers to have infected his Church
in its very institution by Henry VIII. The priest requires a scape-
goat. "Among all the princes who ever reigned in the world, there
was never so infernal a beast as Henry VIII in every vice of the
most odious kind, without any one appearance of virtue." Among
Henry's "detestable crimes," he "cut off the head of Thomas More,
a person of the greatest virtue this kingdom ever produced." In
the Third Voyage of *Gulliver's Travels* More emerges from the

"A Voyage to Nowhere with Thomas More and Jonathan Swift: *Utopia* and
The Voyage to the Houyhnhnms," by John Traugott. From *The Sewanee Review*, LXIX, No. 4 (Autumn 1961), 534-565. Copyright © 1961 by The University
of the South. Reprinted by permission of the author and *The Sewanee Review*.

miasma of history even more brilliantly—indeed, beatifically, one could say, had not Swift followed the Church of Henry, the "supreme head" who martyred More, against the Church of More which was to canonize him. Such is the confusion of loyalties which bedevils men who ask real questions. More appears in the Lucianic dialogue of the dead in Glubbdubdrib the only modern and the only Christian among a sextumvirate of worthies (Brutus, Junius Epaminondas, Cato the Younger, Socrates, and More), a lonely little band of resisters to tyranny. "All the ages of the world cannot add a seventh": does the author modestly nominate himself?

More is White, Henry Black in Swift's universal morality play. History, as usual for Swift, a pageant of symbolic figures, has conveniently juxtaposed Henry and More to divide between them the philosophical universe: More's Socratic irony, rationalism, and catholic ideal of society mock Henry's tyrannical self-sufficiency, mystical nationalism, and private plunder. Similar evaluations of Black and White quicken Swift's irony in his tracts and satires. Like More a "catholic" personality, Swift discovered in the figure of a "true-blue protestant" a walking symbol of the contemporary cant of nationalism, sectarianism, and individualism. "In nothing is the likeness [of Swift to More] more strong," writes R. W. Chambers, More's biographer, "than in the passion shown by Swift against the futile wars of Christian nations which, when narrated, arouse the disgust alike of the virtuous Houyhnhnms and of the magnanimous giants of Brobdingnag. Few things are more remarkable than the salute passed from Jonathan Swift to Thomas More across the two intervening centuries of futile religious strife; it is a sign that, with the cessation of the Wars of Religion, the standpoint of a common European civilization is again becoming intelligible." It is precisely Swift's "catholicism"—not latitudinarianism—in religion and politics, his contempt for nationalism, factionalism, and individualism, that informs the utopian passages of *Gulliver's Travels* and marks its philosophical debt to More.

While detestation of Henry was almost a "party line" of the Augustan High Churchman, Swift's particular opposition of More to Henry points to a conception in the mind of the artist rather than the party man. When Gulliver complains to his Cousin Sympson that some English Yahoos "are so bold as to think my book of travels a mere fiction out of my own brain, and have gone so

ar as to drop hints that the Houyhnhnms and Yahoos have no
nore existence than the inhabitants of Utopia," we smile with
swift the buffoon, but like More Swift played the fool only north-
orthwest, and dead ahead he means to say that the Houyhnhnms
nd Yahoos have the same sort of reality as the inhabitants of
More's *Utopia.* For both *Utopia* and *Gulliver's Travels* are discoveries of the moral and spiritual reality of utopia in our every-
lay lives, and to this end employ as a satiric device a voyager who
s maddened by a glimpse of the reality of the Good in a fantastic
and and of the unreality of everyday life in real Englands. More's
Utopia very possibly suggested to Swift that most essential and
essentially baffling of the satiric effects of *Gulliver's Travels*—Gulliver's utter alienation, his travels done, from the "Yahoo race" and
his contempt for his "visionary scheme" of reforming it. And as
both satires abandon their voyagers at the end in ridiculous pos-
ures of alienation, so they abandon the reader with the burden
of bridging the ironic disjunction between the impossible truth,
utopia, which cannot be ignored, and the shadowy actuality, Eng-
and, which cannot be got rid of.

Two archetypal "solutions" to this puzzle, mutually antagonistic,
though equally unbelievable, hold the field of Swift criticism.
The first is Thackeray's: Swift is a madman, gnashing in the darkness, and therefore at one with Gulliver in his final misanthropy.
While Swift has an obvious right to his poetic madness, surely his
gloom is speciously illuminated in this "solution," for the very
comedy of Gulliver's final posture, as he writes to his Cousin Sympson six months after his *Travels* have failed to correct the world,
returns us to the rational light by which he certainly wrote. On
the other hand, if we pursue to its logical conclusion the view
that Swift is not to be identified with Gulliver we come upon the
other archetypal "solution," equally unconvincing. Here we see
Gulliver, *un grand extravagant,* as Célimène calls Alceste, the object of laughter, having suffered a "bite" (in Augustan slang) by
those ludicrous horses, the Houyhnhnms. By this "solution," Swift
himself becomes that most detested of beings in his private hell,
a modern, who tells us to "adjust" to actuality.[1] This will never do,

---

[1] The "adjustment" thesis takes two forms in recent criticism. One is that of
psychological "adjustment," which Swift is said to recommend to us by making
Gulliver preposterous. Some such formula as, "Thus Swift tells us not to aban-

for Gulliver is alienated for precisely the reason that he is at last
"true-seer"; at least, the scales fallen from his eyes, he sees precisely in the cold crystal of Houyhnhnm reason what Swift's rhetoric during the first three voyages has presented as the truth about
society. We cannot, if Swift is at all right, "adjust" to this actuality: we become decent in failing to do so. What else can Swift's
famous formula, that the sublime point of felicity is to be a fool
among knaves, mean? Are we to reject Gulliver's final noble strictures on imperialism (which are Swift's in other writings)? Shall
we "adjust" to "the sight of a lawyer, a pick-pocket, a colonel, a
fool, a lord, a gamester, a politician, a whore-master, a physician
an evidence . . . a lump of deformity and diseases both in body
and mind smitten with pride?" If Gulliver, finally arrived at the
truth, is now to be revealed to us as merely ridiculous and if his
horses are a "bite," then Swift has inanely piled irony upon irony
in a series of clever reversals until we have a world without meaning, or at best a Mandevillian world in which private vices, if not
public benefits, are the condition of an agreeable society.[2] Such
modern paradox is not Swift's. His own alienation and disaffection
are evident enough to the reader. In his own dreadful phrase, he
was, in the Irish tracts, administering "a dose for the dead," and
his "Thoughts" contain the ominous stricture, that "the want of
a belief is a defect which ought to be concealed when it cannot be
overcome." Gulliver the alienated man was one face, not a mask,
of Jonathan Swift.

These two archetypal "solutions" then belie Swift, both the
artist and the man. More's *Utopia* provides a model of another
sort of "solution" which distinguishes Swift from Gulliver without
denying their close relationship. It is a question of a peculiar point
of view which Swift shared with More, a peculiar kind of irony.

don the whole man for the reason," is usually offered. The other, a refinement
on the first, is that of religious "adjustment." In this extrapolation of the text
the Houyhnhnms represent dry rationalism, deism, or Bolingbroke (or all three);
the Yahoos, original sin or the "flesh"; Gulliver, a soul suffering spiritual dryness
returned by the Grace of God to human compassion. The foundation of this
argument appears to be that, as a priest, Swift *must* have intended such a moral.
Both theses are a "nice" academic rehabilitation of Swift so that he no longer
is torn by savage indignation. He is now "well-adjusted" to the compromises of
his age. The common reader must decide whether Swift was an "adjusted"
clergyman or a passionate and often alienated soul.

[2] Martin Price makes this point in his study, *Swift's Rhetorical Art.*

II. *Irony: The Drama Being Played*

Thomas More heard in his head a speculative philosopher whom he called "Raphael Hythloday" in the book *Utopia*. He was More-the-utopian, an abstract philosopher, whom More-the-politician, a worldly man, as well as More-the-saint, an other-worldly man, often heard. A Renaissance voyager, Hythloday has discovered a world of nowhere, Utopia, a Circe of the reason, that has changed him from a good seafarer into an immobile, absolute utopian. An honest man, Hythloday becomes almost comic as he unpacks his sovereign, absolute remedies to a world that is not there. In fact far more than ordinarily sane, he has satisfied himself that among all men he is uniquely so. More-the-politician tells Hythloday in effect that he should play the fool rather than be one, that he should fit his truth to the drama being played. But Hythloday scorns his advice and *will* be the uniquely sane man. "There is no place," he replies bitterly to More-the-politician, "for philosophy in the councils of princes." "Yes there is," More answers,

> but not for the speculative philosophy which thinks all things suitable for all occasions. There is another philosophy that is more urbane, that takes its proper cue and fits itself to the drama being played, acting its part aptly and well. This is the philosophy you should use. When one of Plautus's comedies is being played and the slaves are joking together, what if you should suddenly appear on the stage in a philosopher's garb and repeat Seneca's speech to Nero from the *Octavia*? Would it not be better to say nothing than to make a silly tragicomedy by mixing opposites? You ruin a play when you add irrelevant and jarring speeches, even if they are better than the play. So go through with the drama in hand as best you can, and do not spoil it because another more pleasing comes into your mind.
>
> So it is in a commonwealth and in the councils of princes. If evil opinions cannot be quite rooted out, and if you cannot correct habitual attitudes as you wish, you must not therefore abandon the commonwealth.[3]

[3] Quotations are from the translation by H. V. C. Ogden.

More is prophesying the pattern of his own life. Against his sanest instincts he elected a few years later to serve Henry VIII. And when eventually he could no longer fit his truth to the drama being played, he added a jarring (and to Henry, irrelevant) speech —and the game was up. An ironist in the well of his being, More throughout his life acted and spoke from this double perspective on reality: of the drama which must be played and of final things which define that drama. He tried to make life a comedy that comes out "right" by working each actor, including himself, in his proper role. In tribute to this man who knew how to play the fool to serve justice, Erasmus gave his great satire a punning title which says it all: *Encomium Moriae*, "The Praise of Folly, or the Praise of More." "Yet why do I say these things to you," he addresses More, "an advocate so distinguished that you can defend in the best way even causes not the best? Farewell, learned More, and doughtily defend your Moria." Folly later uses almost the same figure as More does to describe the dilemma of truth in this world:

> If a person were to try stripping the disguises from actors while they play a scene upon the stage, showing to the audience their real looks and the faces they were born with, would not such a one spoil the whole play. . . ?
>
> The actor who played a woman would now be seen a man; he who a moment ago appeared young, is old; he who but now was a king, is suddenly an hostler; and he who played the god is a sorry little scrub. Destroy the illusion and any play is ruined. It is the paint and trappings that take the eyes of spectators. Now what else is the whole life of mortals but a sort of comedy, in which the various actors, disguised by various costumes and masks, walk on and play each one his part, until the manager waves them off the stage? Moreover, this manager frequently bids the same actor go back in a different costume, so that he who has but lately played the king in scarlet now acts the flunkey in patches. Thus all things are presented by shadows; yet this play is put on in no other way.
>
> But suppose right here some wise man who has dropped down from the sky should suddenly confront me and cry out that the person whom the world has accepted as god and master is not even a man because he is driven sheep-like by his passions. Or again suppose that the visitor should command someone mourning his father's death to laugh, because now his father has really begun to live—for in a sense our earthly life is but a kind of death. Suppose him to address another

who is glorying in his ancestry and to call him low and base born
because he is so far from virtue, the only true fount of nobility.
Suppose him to speak of others in that vein. I ask you what would
he get by it except to be considered by everyone as insane and raving?

The parallel of this foolish wise man dropped down from the
sky to strip the masks from impostors with Hythloday back from
Utopia and with Gulliver furnished with wisdom by the celestial
Houyhnhnms, is obvious. The foolish wise man is wise in his true
understanding of the ideal measure of the drama of actuality, and
he is foolish not to find his rightful part in that drama being played.
The peculiar kind of irony to which this view gives rise is very
likely to be confused with either cynicism or Mandevillian paradox. As public men More and Swift were particularly liable to
such slurs.

If, for example, we read Swift's "Sentiments of a Church of
England Man" as the definition of his religion, as most biographers
do, we lose the man in his role in the drama then being put on. He
is there the conciliator of an audience far gone into the zany
secularism he parodies in the "Argument against Abolishing Christianity." But in "Remarks upon a Book Intituled 'The Rights
of the Christian Church,'" written the same year but never published in his lifetime, his attitude is almost medieval, as he destroys the liberal, vulgarian ethic of Tindall the intellectual fop
whose argument, to put it briefly, is that the Church is, as it
ought to be, by Royal appointment, opium monger to the masses.
Here Swift defends the independence of the Church as a society
from the State. So we have in the "Sentiments" the Church politician cannily shoring up the visible Establishment and in the
"Remarks" the pietist rejecting the State, the actual and the ideal,
both the expression of the same year of his life. And out of his
double view comes the complex irony of one of the great satires,
"An Argument against Abolishing Christianity," in which a brilliant mimicry of inanely smart freethinkers creates an implicit
apology for both the political and spiritual integrities of the
Church.

The comic voices of everyday life were Swift's particular pleasure
—he mimics them in every casual moment—but even these idle-
hour comedians assume very often an unnerving significance simply
because his habitual irony nervously insinuates the ideal into the

everyday comedy. This habit of mind in fact probably accounts for the failure of readers to give his otherwise happy comic spirit its due. One severe critic remarks that his laughter is like the bloodcurdling single Ha! which a Prussian officer permits himself. It is even so in his casual, whimsical irony: "I am now returning to the noble scene of Dublin," he writes a friend, ". . . for fear of burying my parts, to signalize myself among curates and vicars and correct all corruptions crept in relating to the weight of bread and butter through these domains I govern." This seemingly rueful whimsy the addicted reader of Swift feels as something like this: "Though English tyranny has made Irish affairs wholly senseless, I intend to see that butter buyers get true weight, for after all a statesman is only a tradesman with his thumb on the balance. I deserve superior marks for recognizing this obvious metaphor." The Drapier seems to lurk in the wings ready to reduce the government to idiocy.

"More," writes Chambers, "and Socrates are two of the greatest masters of irony who ever lived. (Small wonder that both were admired by that great ironist Jonathan Swift, a man not given to excessive admiration.) More had a habit of uttering his deepest convictions in a humorous way, and his wildest jokes with a solemn countenance. That was the *festivitas* which his friends noted as his most marked characteristic. He gives his own account of it when he makes a friend say to him, 'Ye use to look so sadly when ye mean so merrily, that many times men doubt whether ye speak in sport, when ye mean good earnest.' "

As an old man, replotting in his "cursed" Dublin the world before the Fall—of the Queen's Last Ministry—, Swift was nearly everyday the object of outrageous flattery by his English correspondents. Their letters suggest to him that he is at least the Irish Cid, the English Herodotus, and the retired Machiavel of the Western World. Actually, of course, where Swift acted a part in English or Irish affairs he did just that—*acted a part* that was not Jonathan Swift *in propria persona* but a player like the Examiner or the Drapier, to say nothing of his pirouettes on the literary stage as an absolutely indescribable fool in *A Tale of a Tub* and the most complicated simpleton in *Gulliver*. Perhaps the tribute most flattering to his histrionic soul was a letter from his friend William King, Principal of St. Mary's College, Oxford, who wrote, "If you accept of this invitation, I promise to meet you at Chester, and to conduct you to King Edward's lodgings, and then St. Mary Hall may boast of a triumvirate that is not to be matched in any part of the world, Sir Thomas More, Erasmus, and the Drapier." The comparison is not merely rhetorical. Swift was not the "saviour of his nation," a great historian, or a *politique,* but he was a great ironist who knew how to find out the truth by acting in the drama being played.

No ironist of this sort could go in for political absolutism. Among Swift's obsessions was the linguistic process by which tyrants destroy the meanings of words; he must have been fascinated by Henry VIII's genius in using the title "Defender of the Faith" indifferently, whether the faith was Roman or Anglican. A tyrant can reduce life to insane paradox: his graciousness, Swift shows in his portrait of the King of Luggnagg, is an expedient mitigation of his cruelty; his justice, his discrimination among his victims; and his mercy, his indifference. Anything can mean anything. More's and Swift's irony on the other hand makes distinctions. In *Four Last Things* More likens the King to the silly player who becomes proud of the lord's gay golden gown he wears in a stage-play. How else can one defend himself from implication in tyranny —of either absolutism or liberalism, the two beasts in the Swiftian political jungle—save by acting in the drama being played and yet looking on the play with an immovable utopia in the back of the head?

III. *The Utopian Mentality of More and Swift*

Utopia is nowhere but in the mind, which is free of space and time. It is not a rationalization of what exists (i.e., a conservative mystique), nor an historical dialectic (communism, Christianity), nor a program for the future ("progress," liberalism). Its only function is to measure the present by an unchangeable ideal. Once we moderns have mastered this uncongenial idea, it becomes somewhat less burdensome for an apologist to confess that More's Utopians and Swift's Houyhnhnms are an impossibly dull lot. In Utopia there is all the verve of a modern suburban development built on a rectilinear street plan, with rectilinear thoughts, people, and houses. The figure is just, for in contrast to the sixteenth century European cities More knew, which appear to us romantic and were in fact the product of the exigencies and fancies of succeeding ages and peoples, those in Utopia are squarely planned and laid out, once and for all, for predetermined people of predetermined "habits." But as everyone knows, only unplanned cities are interesting.

Utopia was born rectilinear in More's mind. It has no past and no future. Nothing will ever change. True, there was an eponymous Utopus who like Lycurgus lived and established things once upon a time forevermore, but by fiat, and so in effect Utopia has no history. The Utopians are exactly what Utopus was. The Houyhnhnms similarly have no history. There was not even a great horse once upon a time.

One of the reasons Swift considers More the only modern fit company for the ancients in his Empyrean is that he is an ancient in his mental construction. In his *Idea of Progress,* J. B. Bury contrasts to the idea of progress the "ancient" attitude towards change:

> The theories of Plato are only the most illustrious example of the tendency characteristic of Greek philosophical thinkers to idealise the immutable as possessing a higher value than that which varies. This affected all their social speculations. They believed in the ideal of an absolute order in society, from which, when it is once established, any deviation must be for the worse. This prejudice against change excluded the apprehension of civilization as a progressive movement. It did not occur to Plato or any one else that a perfect order might be attainable by a long series of changes and adaptations. Such an order, being an embodiment of reason could be created only by a deliberate and immediate act of the planning mind.

The idea of progress, Bury continues, is characteristic of the moderns and absolutely unthinkable for the ancients. Since the Utopians and the Houyhnhnms live by absolute reason, "progress" and indeed change—even geographical change—are unthinkable.

Domestic removals in Utopia are conducted on the principle of the game of Musical Chairs. Householders every ten years change houses by lot, and, of course, all houses are the same. And should one remove to another city, all fifty-four of those are built on a common plan. Country mice and city mice are even the same people, for everyone does a regular two-year turn in a farm commune. Probably given pause by their Christianity, neither More nor Swift can allow Plato's community of wives, but both Utopians and Houyhnhnms mate eugenically and distribute children equitably according to sex and number. All this geometric rationalism in Utopian life is unsullied by disagreement, and therefore, as among the Houyhnhnms, the axioms never fail.

Though this uniformity of life may suggest to us a hideous "conformism" which only the marriage of American Suburbia with a totalitarian police state could hope to achieve, in fact it is not "conformism" at all but reason which rules Utopia, however indistinguishable the two conditions of life may appear. As the heliotrope to the sun, is each rational will in Utopia to justice. We are not in any sense then in an authoritarian or conformistic community, but More and Swift would say that the confusion is very likely with those who consider freethinking thinking and freedom freethinking. If one is a Platonist, as was More, reason cannot be consistent with freethinking since there is only one reason. The Houyhnhnms also "agree entirely with the sentiments of Socrates" as to the distinction between reason and opinion.

But what does "reason" mean? Obviously, if one lays out streets and houses and gardens and water systems and even the lives of the people, it is for some end. That end in Utopia is the satisfaction of human nature. "There is enough of everything, and no fear that anyone will claim more than he needs. Why should anyone be suspected of asking for more than is necessary when there is never any shortage? Men and animals alike are greedy and rapacious from fear of want. Only human pride glories in surpassing others in conspicuous consumption. For this kind of vice there is no room whatsoever in the Utopian way of life." All this sounds startlingly modern until we come to the alien note of "pride," alien at least to a modern socialist. "What may seem strange," says Hythloday, "they seek support for their pleasure philosophy from religion, which is serious and forbidding." It is in fact a system in which there exists a complete interpenetration of politics and religion and metaphysics, of the physical and the spiritual, of the state and the church.

The attention to the needs of human nature in this world, what the Utopians call "pleasure," is directed by a metaphysics borrowed almost directly from Plato's *Philebus*. In this dialogue, after Philebus has proposed innocently that pleasure is the end of life, Socrates with great pleasure ties him and his friend Protarchus into dialectical knots until they admit that the life of unconscious pleasure is the life of an oyster. They plead with Socrates to stop puzzling them. "We must keep up our spirits," says Socrates to the two oysters. He proceeds to use Philebus's original premise in a way he never imagined. Pleasure is not to be despised, says Socrates, but put in its place, and in its place the hierarchy of pleasures must be determined. There are the pleasures, for example, of scratching, of sounds, and of knowledge. Of course Socrates comes to the point that the highest pleasure only points to higher goods, which reason will tell us are beauty, symmetry, and truth. But in order to make such a distinction of the goods we must seek the mingled experiences of life, praying by the way to the "god of mingling," "if any of us is to find his way home." The Utopians have found the way home and so do not need any mingled experiences. That is why they are dull. The Houyhnhnms, though they have no metaphysics, have always been at home with reason, which is their highest pleasure, and so they too are dull.

Utopia's Platonic religion is not deism or latitudinarianism, the fond dream of the Cambridge Platonists in the next century. While Utopia's human benignity and justice depend upon reason, irrationality (including irrational "dissent") is punished by death. Public good, determined by rational principles, is the highest virtue. One thinks of how the Houyhnhnms skin the irrational Yahoos and put Gulliver to sea in a small boat for the crime of possessing an irrational human nature. In the *Utopia* More writes a myth of an integral national state and church, a myth which heralds and gives some definition to a period in English history in which the church could sometimes be described simply as "Erastian." At the very close of this period Swift stands, a dispossessed seneschal looking homeward to More. Defying logic, Englishmen during these two centuries gave their devotion—though often, too, only their lip-service—to a catholic religion impossibly allied to a fierce nationalism. After Queen Anne, with the fall of the last Tory ministry, the ideal of a catholic church and a national state is hardly more than sentimentality bordering on treason. No fanciful embellishment of Swift's character could be more fantastic than the mere truth, that his entire life was dominated by an anachronistic—"romantic," one would say, were the word allowed in the purlieus of Swift's critics—an anachronistic allegiance to the idea of an Anglo-Catholic church, Anglo-Catholic not in the present ritualistic sense of the term, but in the Laudian sense of a church integral with the society.

Cranmer told More that Henry's power was the condition of life, but Tudor divinity was itself subject to the growth of agrarian capitalism. And to this force too Swift was doctrinally hostile, almost as though he were a man of More's own time. The wealth of the Church was the bribe by which Henry VIII secured his supreme authority in Church and State: it created a class of private landowners responsible neither to the feudal system nor to the Church. Only a step farther was the enclosure of public lands by private wealth and the turning of agrarian feudalism to agrarian capitalism. A principal thesis of Tawney's *Religion and the Rise of Capitalism* is that "the classes whose backing was needed to make the Reformation a political success, had sold their support on terms which made it inevitable that it should be a social disaster." It is of the pauperized Englishmen, the beggars and derelicts resulting from Henry's policy that Hythloday speaks in first proposing his Utopia. More is a "communist" because for him collectivism is the answer of the Christian humanist to both authoritarianism and capitalism, the one vitiating the rule of reason, and the other, the mystique of the common body.

Hythloday in his passionate peroration contrasts the principle of the common good by which the Utopians live with the aggressive individualism of Europeans. "In other places, when they speak of the common good, every man is looking for his own good. But in Utopia where there is no private property and where they zealously pursue the public business, there the name commonwealth is doubly deserved. Elsewhere, even though the state is prosperous most men know that they may die of hunger if they do not look out for themselves, and so they are forced to take care of themselves rather than other people. In Utopia where everything belongs to everybody they know that if the public warehouses and granaries are full, no one will lack anything for his personal use." As Swift sets his idiot Yahoos to hiding shining stones in the dirt, so More has his rational Utopians scorn gold except as a badge of idiocy for slaves.

Because we today consider social justice an economic and political matter, More's Utopia is too often taken as programmatic. But when at last Hythloday concludes his dream vision we discover that neither the economic system nor the political accounts for that "conspiracy of the rich, who pursue their own agrandizement under the name and title of the commonwealth," but rather "that one monster pride, the first and foremost of all evils," which "measures her property not by her goods but by others' wants." And we are left at the end with More's strange combination of moral will with social action.

Had conditions changed so little in England in the two centuries between More and Swift that Hythloday's bitter speeches—on dispossessed beggars and thieves, enclosures, attrition of Church responsibility, and the growth of private venture—seem anachronistically an echo of Swift's? It is a symbolic recasting of history, and the reader rightly asks what philosophical view gives coherence to Swift's seemingly hysterical hatred of contemporary life. We do know that he considered history only a moral drama put on by the sorcerers of Glubbdubdrib in which a few heroes and demigods stand in counterview to a rout of "pedlars, pick-pockets, highwaymen and bullies."

While Swift's tracts on beggars and cottiers, weavers and mercenaries, English woolens and English bishops seem often merely splenetic, they all picture an incoherent society; and the image of the dispossessed, of ravening beggars, thieves, and cottiers, occupies in Swift's *imagination* the crucial position it does in More's. The Irish tracts call up the ghost of a common political and religious body to look on the insane factions and insane free entrepreneurs, bankers, foreign adventurers, and rack-renters. Irish land was not used as the common wealth, to sustain Irishmen, but as capital for investors. Fertile farms were turned into sheep walks and the population dispossessed, and to add insult to injury, under the mercantile system the woolens were required to be spun in England. "We are worse," Swift writes, "than the condition of Arachne because our vitals are extracted but we are not allowed to spin them." While quite conscious as a political realist that he was administering "a dose for the dead," he imagined an Irish commonwealth, equally with England under Church and King.

Equally naïve, as naïve as More's, are Swift's notions on war. The Utopians, who have a citizen army and despise imperialism, "consider nothing so inglorious as the glory won in war." This is a rather daring apothegm for More who later said that certainly Henry loved him but if his head were put in balance against just one of the many castles in France which Henry hoped to win, why, then

his head would go. Even more daring is Swift's echo of this senti-
ment, for in the eighteenth century, England was not likely to
pursue any other course than that of national glory. His contempt
for English arms, and his slander of Marlborough border on treason.
Not only does Blefuscu (France) come off more honorably than
Lilliput (England), but the *Travels* as a whole present a picture of
"glory" which is at worst insane tyranny and at best absurd postur-
ing. And the last chapter of the fourth voyage is an indictment of
imperialism that can only be interpreted as an assault by a disaffected subject on English national policy. Like the Utopians (and
the King of Brobdingnag) Swift can see no use for a standing army
except to support tyranny at home and adventure abroad. More
proposes a naïve alternative to imperialism. Hythloday tells the
story of the Acorians, who having conquered another kingdom
found themselves continually putting down rebellions, protecting
the people against invaders, increasing their taxes, spilling their
blood for the king's "glory," acquiring a taste for plunder and
violence, and allowing their own liberties and laws to fall into
contempt. They decide on the expedient—so obvious as to be brilliant—of coming home and minding their own business. Gulliver's
naïveté in his final alienation, is, like Hythloday's, simply revolutionary as he cuts through the moral grotesquerie of English
polichinelles. If one is not to be corrupt, More and Swift obviously
believed, then one must be simple-minded.

The moral superiority of the public good over personal and the
mutual subjection of the members of the commonwealth, King,
landlord, peasant, trader, priest, are almost the only principles of
Swift's political philosophy.[4] Emotional overtones—dissenters ought
to be "persecuted," bankers hanged, kings and bishops sneered at,
and similar flourishes of the lance—never take him far from funda-

---

[4] Swift's commentators have rightly emphasized his attachment to the classical
ideal of a balance of powers in a mixed polity of king, aristocracy, and commons,
but Swift's emphasis is not upon a mechanical balance or stalemate but upon
"mutual subjection." "Balance" for him carries no sense of the free enterprise
of each faction. The contemporary threats to "mutual subjection" (Swift's own
term)—individualism, faction, secularism, "liberalism," and the "money interest"
—are the real objects of his attack in both the tracts and the satires. "The *vox
populi*," he early wrote, in "Contests and Dissensions," "ought to be understood
of the universal bent and current of the people." The same conviction, which
is hardly derived from the balance of power theory, underlies the argument of
the "Fourth Drapier's Letter."

mentals. Their best explicit statement is in the sermons, "The Duty of Mutual Subjection" and "On the Martyrdom of King Charles I." In Lilliput's original constitution, in Brobdingnag, and in the land of the Houyhnhnms, this collectivistic attitude is given mythical figurations. Like More's communism, Swift's principle of "mutual subjection" is an argument against individualism and for the common body.

One of Swift's most ostentatious quarrels in his religious tracts is with the late politician Henry VIII over Henry's despoliation of the monasteries. What R. W. Chambers calls Henry's "vulgarity" in claiming to be the founder of hospitals which he merely did not confiscate is already depicted in Book I of Utopia, many years before, where Hythloday pictures the king's sycophantic counsellors egging him on to "use" Church endowments. But why should Swift have concerned himself about Henry's seizures—so long an accomplished fact that the most respectable families in England were then living from their endowments? No one would think of upbraiding Jane Austen for her callousness or irreligion in putting a genteel country family in the stolen property of Northanger Abbey. The cause seemed indeed well-lost by the eighteenth century and Swift's indignation a romantic affectation which makes Johnson's toasts to the Stuarts seem hard-headed. But no—in "An Essay on the Fates of Clergyman" Swift discovers that the universal English contempt for the Church, symbolized in his portrait of the scrubby, main-chancing clergyman who sits like a servant on the edge of the squire's chair, is attributable in part to the Church's contemptible poverty, commencing with Henry's lust. It is as though Henry had licensed landlords who refuse tithes, impropriate church lands, and secure confiscatory leaseholds from corrupt bishops. A vast simplification of Church history, but Swift cared only for symbols and Henry is his symbol. A contemptible and time-serving clergy might present a decent figure and resist secularization of its functions if it had sufficient funds to take care of itself. It was an axiom for Swift, a tautology perceived by no one. Henry VIII lived in Swift's eighteenth century because Swift needed a symbol that would explain land-capitalism which fed squires and landlords (usually absentee) and bishops (almost always absentee) and did not feed priests and peasants (always present). Like More he considered that society might provide something, enough, for all. The Modest Proposer has the same notion, but he, being practical, works with the facts of modern life.

If reason is to control our way of life, that reason is more than X an empirical guide; it is a teleology. The Brobdingnagians and the Houyhnhnms do not reason pragmatically; they are horrified by the violation of the principles of order, justice, and nature. If human life is directed by its end, how can secular and religious directions differ? Utopus was neither dogmatic nor tyrannical, says Hythloday, but he expected all Utopians as rational beings to live by the established religion, for Utopian "freedom" is a Platonic inner harmony deriving from reason. If a Utopian does not accept the established religion, which is broadly defined, he is given short shrift. "He [Utopus] deemed it foolish and insolent for anyone to try to make all men accept his own beliefs by force and by threats. If one religion is true and the others false he clearly foresaw that the truth would prevail by its own strength. But if men fight and riot, as evil and headstrong men will do, then the best and holiest religion in the world will be crowded out by the emptiest superstitions, like wheat choked by thorns and briars."

As much as he believed in free will, More's last thought would be the liberal notion that truth will prevail if only the unfettered gladiators of faction are put into the public arena to chop one another down to the same lumpy shapes. Now it is remarkable that these strange (strange for us moderns) principles establishing the relation between church and state in Utopia are exactly those Swift —if we judge from many tracts and from *Gulliver*—would have maintained in England. "[The Brobdingnagian King] laughed at my odd kind of arithmetic (as he was pleased to call it) in reckoning the number of our people by a computation drawn from the several sects among us in religion and politics. He said, he knew no reason why those who entertain opinions prejudicial to the public, should be obliged to change, or should not be obliged to conceal them. And it was tyranny in any government to require the first, so it was weakness not to enforce the second: for a man may be allowed to keep poisons in his closet, but not to vend them about for cordials." Swift shares More's faith that only sour factionalism can withstand the ceremony of the establishment if wrangling (in Burke's phrase, the "dissonance of dissent") is kept down. He leaves, however, the same possibility as More for change and for the practice of private worship. Both More and Swift demand "freedom of religion" in their sense—freedom for the Church and its members to carry their religion into civil affairs. Neither would consider the Church as other than under a state of persecution in our century when it does not enjoy such freedom of action. This is the substance of Swift's denial that he was a party man while he supported so virulently the virulent church party.

It is impossible not to be impressed by the correspondence of Swift's thought to More's. The evidence that he drew heavily from More is overwhelming: his imitation of parts of *Utopia* in Gulliver, his homage to More, and finally, perhaps most important, his participation in the same intellectual, political, and religious cause to which More became a martyr. Perhaps most striking is the similarity in their political habits. Both practical politicians, who knew how to live with the compromises of their ages, they nevertheless performed upon a moral tightrope by maintaining an utopia in the back of the head as a measure of those compromises. What one can insist upon then is not the specific schemes in *Utopia* which correspond to this or that of Swift's anachronistic notions, but the whole mad vision of utopia which lies behind his passion and More's.

IV. *A Formal Aspect of* Utopia *and of* Gulliver's Travels

Any casual reader can see that Gulliver is, after all, not a horse; the only problem is to see why Swift should have obliged him to imagine that he is. That the two pervasive critical "solutions"— "Swift is Gulliver" and "Gulliver is ridiculous"—are directly contradictory is itself a critical consideration of importance and an ironic testimony to Swift's peculiar irony. Let us now notice more particularly the device—the alienated Gulliver—by which this irony is expressed. As we have seen, *Utopia* employs a similar device.

Utopia is cast in the guise of a conversation between Thomas More, the King's diplomatic emissary to Holland, a Dutch friend, and his friend, a mad mariner named Raphael Hythloday. Hythloday has sailed the seas and discovered that his real home is "nowhere," a country called "Utopia." The two activities, mariner and philosopher, are not merely metaphorically related in the Renaissance. More considers Hythloday's desire to explore real oceans with Americus Vespucius inseparable from his absolute devotion to philosophy. More's *Utopia* appeared only a decade after Americus's *Four Voyages*. Plato, Ulysses, Americus, Hythloday—they were all one to More. Like Swift, who seems to confuse Henry VIII with Walpole, More cared for "history" as an allegorical drama in which certain individuals happened to play certain roles always well known to the mind that examines life.

For the instruction of his own age, to contrast a modern journalistic view of history as "facts" to his own as allegory or exemplum, Swift dresses up More's Hythloday to look like Defoe's Robinson Crusoe. The result is a Gulliver-as-Crusoe who discovers senseless facts until in the Fourth Voyage, as Hythloday, he discovers a fixed idea by which to measure those facts. One might imagine a Janus-figure called "Swift-Defoe" at the gateway to the Augustan age, the Swift face looking backward, snapping like a Cerberus at anyone who merely wants to look in on the modern world, the Defoe face like yesterday's newspaper spilling out endless facts about it.

The other major figure in the conversation, "More," is a worldly philosopher who by some prescience knows instinctively what Hythloday was searching out but is committed to living in this world. He thinks that Hythloday should come out from under his bushel to bear his torch into the councils of princes, which will at least make the darkness visible. Another speaker is Peter Giles, a cultivated man who lends the conversation his air of worldly *savoir-faire*. Within the frame of the dialogue, Hythloday gives an account of his visit to England, in which Cardinal Morton, obviously an *éminence grise* projection of "More," appears. Hythloday is an honest man dazzled by his own virtue; "More" (with Morton), a philosopher descended to the marketplace to see what he can do to relate the one to the many; Giles, a decent man of this world who considers that European civilization is not negligible. We have in effect a Platonic dialogue which explores the possibility of justice in the everyday world.

Thomas More's decision to fit himself to "the drama being played" in England, the course "More" of the *Utopia* recommends to Hythloday, his friend Erasmus accepts not as fatal to More, which in fact it was, but as a loss to comedy: "I should regret what has happened to More, who has been drawn into court life, were it not that under such a King, and with so many learned colleagues it seems rather a university than a court; still, we shall get no more news from Utopia to make us laugh, and I know that More would rather laugh than be carried in official state." Obviously to Erasmus, Utopia is not solemnly programmatic. In the absolute monarchy of England where things were hardly utopian in anybody's sense, the element of foolery in a courtier's projected utopia must have been evident. Had More's communism been a trumpet of a Joshua before the Tower of London, he would have indeed needed the hand of God to save him.

Nevertheless the implications of *Utopia* are clearly inimical to Henry, and More nearly saved himself and nearly made a philosopher of the King in the way he recommends to Hythloday—by playing the fool. In the *Utopia* he carries the principles in which he believed to their logical, and so farcical, extreme, so that no one could accept them "seriously." Furthermore he uses a system of value which is obviously incomplete. The Christian virtues of Faith, Hope, and Charity hover doubtfully in the background of *Utopia*'s classical virtues, like tutelary spirits uncertain of their duties. One sort of love only, the Platonic Eros, is present in Utopia. Of the personal life of the Utopians we hear nothing. Of personal salvation, of Providence, of the Grace which enables faith—of these Christian concerns in the nonpublic life of the individual, we hear nothing. More's own life and his other works show that he did not believe that human life was or could or should be anything like this. He simply subjects European life to the criticism of Platonic rationalism, as Swift in his Brobdingnag and Houyhnhnm utopias subjects it to the criticism of his sort of rationalism. Every citizen of Utopia is a Platonist. Utopia, to effect its purpose, must be nowhere.

But to the modern communist More's Utopia is somewhere. He would hardly interest himself in the Platonic rationalization for Utopia's pleasure ethic. In *Thomas More and his Utopia*, Karl Kautsky, a communist, attributes More's prescience in envisioning modern socialism to the peculiar influence of oppressive material conditions upon a great humanist and humanitarian mind. These conditions were nationalistic conflicts fostered by the growth of international trade and the dispossession of the poor by agricultural capitalism. Because the material means to proletarian power did not exist, More was forced to follow a Catholic will-o'-the-wisp in which he did not really believe.

This critique of *Utopia* leaves out several factors in More's conception, which happen to be crucial. The first is that More envisions not material pleasure as the end of his society but a metaphysical justice. Every man a philosopher, says More. Secondly, More's anti-capitalism derives from his notion that justice depends upon a society which is a common body. *Utopia* does not look forward programmatically; it looks backward mythically to old principles, to the corporate ideal of medieval Christianity, and the justice of Plato's *Republic*.

In defining the idea of progress, J. B. Bury makes a distinction between two kinds of utopia, which is useful in placing More among the nonliteralists of the imagination who founded cities of the mind without attempting to re-establish Eden. Bacon, in distinction to Plato and More, projects a doctrine of social utility as the end of knowledge, so that by implication all human effort looks toward a millennium when the nature of man will be "cured" and there will be a terrestrial city paradise. Plato and More on the other hand would consider this doctrine trivial. "The heads of Plato's city are metaphysicians, who regulate the welfare of the people by abstract doctrines established once and for all; while the important feature of the *New Atlantis* is the college of scientific investigators, who are always discovering new truths which may alter the conditions of life." The idea of progress ironically reverses the meaning of Utopia —"nowhere"—to "somewhere."

As Karl Mannheim in his *Ideology and Utopia* puts it, "The great utopias do not confound the ideal with the reality. For them the ideal and the real remain irreconcilable. So there are no happy endings in the greater utopias but there cannot be any despair either, because the real remains inviolate." And Socrates, who always resorted to myth when reason led him beyond actuality, answers the objection, "The city whose foundation we have been describing, has its being in words: for there is no spot on earth, I imagine, where it exists," "No, but perhaps it is laid up in heaven as a pattern for him who wills to see, and seeing, to found a city in himself. Whether it exists anywhere or ever will exist is no matter." The visions of Socrates, of More, and of Swift have the double perspective of comedy and idealism. Ruskin ticked it off exactly: "What an infinitely wise—infinitely foolish—book *Utopia* is; making its own wisdom folly for evermore." More conceived this perplexing book, and Swift read it, as the wisdom of folly. *Utopia* is poetry, just as the myth of the *Phaedrus* is poetry, and Sidney who called the poet the "creator of another nature," understood this: ". . . what philosopher's counsel can so readily direct a prince, as the feigned

Cyrus in Xenophon, . . . as Aeneas in Virgil; or as a whole commonwealth, as the ways of Sir Thomas More in his Utopia?"

Because they both thought of reality as transcending the actual,
More and Swift liked to mix realism with fantasy. This is of course
the basic literary technique of the *Utopia* and of *Gulliver,* and this
technique symbolizes More's and Swift's notion of reality. More
prefaces his *Utopia* with a realistic dialogue on the ways of the
world which takes place in the home of a real man (Peter Giles) in
a real city (Antwerp) with a real narrator (Thomas More) who is
engaged in a real mission (a commercial treaty for Henry VIII in
Flanders). Moreover, the conversation takes us back to the very real
contemporary affairs in both England and France. No comedy could
be more realistically set. There is only tip-off and that to the
cognoscenti. More was one of the handful of Englishmen of his day
who knew Greek, but the apologist for Utopia, Raphael Hythloday,
we learn, is also "eminently learned in the Greek"; he ought to
know then, as More knows, that his name means "nonsense" and
that *he* does not exist, despite the realism of his setting. But
Hythloday is a terribly passionate man and too preoccupied to
translate his name. More, however, suffers him throughout his long
dialogue to continue under the delusion that he and his ideal commonwealth do actually exist. He represents then those who confuse
the city of the mind with actuality, a confusion, we see, More is
well aware of in the habits of most men.

Literally, Thomas More announces that he is arguing with "Nonsense" but by his earnestness and careful answers he lets us know
that "Nonsense" is well worth arguing with, well worth hearing out.
One reason "Nonsense" is worth hearing is that he has an un-
accountable interest in something that does not at all concern most
"sensible" people—a state well and wisely governed. Practical men,
on the other hand, are mostly interested in "monsters, which are
common enough—Scyllas, ravenous harpies, and cannibals are easy
enough to find anywhere."

In setting "Raphael Nonsense's" fantasy in a realistic frame,
More is playing the fool in a manner that Swift later took as his
own. Swift parodies the fabulous adventure story, turning Ulysses
into that drab fellow, Gulliver—like Hythloday, expert enough at
languages to know what his name means if he would only stop to
think—who discovers those fabulous animals, the Yahoos, in a
fabulous country, only to learn that they too came from England.

Rather than shipwreck our imaginations on Circe's island, Swift suggests that we might discover her pigs in our own parlors. The finding of a "fantastic" truth in everyday life, a truth far more fabulous than "scyllas, ravenous harpies, and cannibals," is certainly Swift's principal satiric device—and philosophic statement. It reveals a notion of reality which, like Plato's and More's, treats everyday life as, finally, an allegory.

In Utopia proper Hythloday (Nonsense) describes the great capital city of Amaurot (dim place), situated on the mighty river Anyder (no water), ruled by a learned Prince Ademus (without a people). And so it goes. We are in Cloud-cuckooland of Aristophanic comedy where the birds have made things at last come out right. Hythloday is a worthy who is absolutely seduced by a vision we know More respects, since it is the measure of European pride. But *Utopia* is a myth in precisely the way that Plato's *Phaedrus* and *Republic* are myths, a symbolic abstraction of certain qualities of life. Utopia is a myth that can make us see that England is—in another sense of the word—a myth. Similarly, out of the most mundane setting, *Gulliver's Travels* develops into one of the weirdest fantasies of our literature, but the fantasy of Houyhnhnmland is an exact measure of everything that the previous voyages have revealed about England. Again, by his technique of mixing realism with fantasy, Swift, like More, is asking us which is the more fantastic, once the scales fall from our—and Gulliver's—eyes, Houyhnhnmland or England.

As Hythloday, prideful, disaffected, Eros-sick, resembles so closely Gulliver at the end of the *Travels,* so is he, as a satiric device, disposed of in much the same manner. Both Hythloday and Gulliver conclude their accounts with denunciations of pride which only an alienated soul could utter. Irony, when it cuts as deeply between appearance and reality as More's and Swift's, is itself the mark of alienation. Irony can run a gamut from mere snobbery (occasionally in Swift's case) to a philosophical distinction of the aristocratic One from the vulgar Many, and perhaps further, to a tragic destruction of the personality of the ironist who cannot bear the loneliness of his own irony. How far the aspect of More's and Swift's personalities represented by Hythloday and Gulliver ruled their personal lives is a biographical question not pertinent to the present discussion, but certainly it is pertinent to note that the alienated philosophers, Hythloday and Gulliver of the fourth voyage, are the very foundations of the ironic views of More and Swift. Since *Utopia* and *Gul-*

liver are rhetorical works, Hythloday and Gulliver remain devices or figures of that rhetoric and one cannot properly speak of them as tragic figures. Nevertheless, for the purpose of emotional urgency they are moved close enough to the status of "round" characters to call up one of the proper themes of tragedy—the virtue that destroys. The strange combination of the tragic and the ridiculous in their final postures is the very condition of life, More and Swift say, for the philosopher in this world. In the *Republic,* Socrates answers Adeimantus's sneer that philosophers have ever been, as everyone knows, the worst sort of governors, by turning the argument around to show that a true philosopher (in Platonic terms, one who loves justice) could not bear the world as it is and would fly mankind. And the prisoner released from the cave, having seen the true light, is considered ridiculous by his erstwhile fellows who are still in chains. Indeed it is hard to imagine a philosopher who loves justice not made mad and ridiculous by the world, unless he be an ironist like Socrates, More, and Swift. And here is precisely the difference between Swift and Gulliver: Gulliver is not an ironist of Swift's sort.

Still, at the end, in his passionate moments, Gulliver is often very like the satirist. Gulliver has now mastered that characteristic Swiftian figure, the undulating coil of vile epithets which reduces all varieties of evil to one category of grotesque idiocy: "Here were no gibers, censurers, backbiters, pickpockets, highwaymen, house-breakers, attorneys, bawds, buffoons, gamesters, politicians, wits, splenetics, tedious talkers, controvertists, ravishers, murderers, rob-bers, virtuosos . . ." Even closer to Swift is his fundamental view of life: "I am not in the least to be provoked at the sight of a lawyer, a pickpocket, a colonel, a fool, a lord, a gamester, a poli-tician, a whore-master, a physician, an evidence, a suborner, an attorney, a traitor, or the like; this is all according to the due course of things: but when I behold a lump of deformity and diseases both in body and mind, smitten with *pride,* it immediately breaks all the measures of my patience. . . ." Thus also is Hythloday to More: "If that one monster pride, the first and foremost of all evils, did not forbid it, the whole world would doubtless have adopted the laws of the Utopians long before this, drawn on by a rational per-ception of what each man's true interest is or else by the authority of Christ our Saviour, who in His great wisdom knows what is best and in His loving kindness bids us do it. . . . Pride is too deeply rooted in men's hearts to be easily torn out. I am glad, therefore, that the Utopians have achieved their social organization, which I wish all mankind would imitate."

But after maneuvering its alienated philosopher into a sympathetic relation to the reader, each work carefully establishes another point of view which controls our attitude toward him. In *Utopia* certainly the figure "More" serves this purpose, for the speaker "More" understands Hythloday and places his truth in the ironic perspective which for More defines the human condition: on the one hand the fixed ideal exists as the reality; on the other the drama of actuality must be played. In *Gulliver* there is no explicit "More" figure. Don Pedro is only a good man who knows no more than the good man Gulliver knew before meeting the Houyhnhnms. He exists to emphasize Gulliver's alienation; he allows Gulliver to make Swift's point that even good Yahoos are Yahoos. Gulliver should know: he himself was expelled from the Houyhnhnms for this reason. But this very impossibility of human life in the country of reason forces the reader to an ironic perspective like that of "More" in *Utopia*. And this irony is underscored by the final comedy of Gulliver's letter to his cousin Sympson and by the slipping mask which reveals Swift, as Gulliver cautions his reader that his noble strictures on imperialism cannot apply to England. Swift then re-emphasizes Gulliver-as-satiric-device almost at the moment he shows us his "round" potentialities as a tragic figure. In this way the satirist turns a restorative irony upon himself without at all abandoning the Gulliver side of his view of life. For without the idealism, mad and ridiculous though it be, of Hythloday and Gulliver, More and Swift would be nihilistic cynics, reducing all human endeavor to mere idiocy. Without the idealism, it is only a step from the "More" who insists that a King's counsellor fit his philosophy "to the drama being played," to, on one extreme, a shifty, time-serving politician, so accommodating that he loses his identity, or on the other, a machiavel for whom any means is justified. At any rate, Thomas More pictures his own implicit corruption in Hythloday's rebuke to "More" for his accommodation:

Suppose the counsellors are discussing how they can raise money for the King's treasury. One man recommends increasing the value of money when the king pays his debts and decreasing it when he collects his revenues. Another proposes a pretense of war that money may be raised to carry it on; then when the money is in, making peace, so that the people will attribute the peace to the piety of their prince and to his tender care for the lives of his subjects. A third calls to mind some old moth-eaten laws, regarded as antiquated by long disuse, forgotten by the king's subjects and consequently broken. He proposes levying the penalties for breaking these laws, so that the king will get a great sum of money as well as credit for executing the law and doing justice. A fourth proposes forbidding many things under severe penalties, especially such as are contrary to the public interest, and then dispensing with these prohibitions for money. By this means the King pleases his people and makes a double profit.

Now what if after this advice was given, I should get up and assert that such counsel was both dishonorable and ruinous to the king?

A man has no chance to do good when his colleagues are more likely to corrupt the best of men than be corrected themselves. He will either be corrupted himself or if he remains sound and innocent he will be blamed for the folly and knavery of others. He is far from being able to mend matters by guiding policy indirectly! That is why Plato in an excellent simile showed that wise men will not meddle in affairs of state.

Hythloday puts the case in exactly Swift's formula (or Swift puts his in More's) that the ordinary choice of life is that of being a fool or a knave. Hythloday's choice is another possibility—proud retirement within himself, since he cannot retire to Nowhere; Gulliver, having been expelled from the wonderful stables of the Houyhnhnms, leaves the Augean stables of the world, which he knows very well now, for a similar retirement. Hythloday says that he has done his duty by his friends and considers that they cannot properly expect more. "The only result of [taking my part in society] will be that while I try to cure others of madness, I myself will rave along with them!"

Curiously, then, the good man somehow allies himself with pride, irresponsibility, and cynicism. With considerably more comedy Swift puts almost the same sentiments as Hythloday's into the mouth of Gulliver in the prefatory letter to his cousin Sympson, where he complains that he has seen his Yahoo corruptions revive since trying to help the human race and announces that now he is done forever with such visionary schemes.

To the two choices of life—to be a fool or knave, or to retire from the human race to Utopia or Houyhnhnmland—More and Swift propose a third: one can live in the world by playing the fool and not being one, by keeping utopia a city of the mind, where Raphael Nonsense and Lemuel Gulliver can live.

Ernst Cassirer, in his *Platonic Renaissance in England,* defines this "third choice" as More's:

> Thomas More stands among the finest and most fertile minds of his epoch, and this intellectual fertility is not free of inner contradictions. All the ideals and all the higher aspirations of the time meet in him. He is a humanist and a practical lawyer, a political mind and a religious thinker, a realistic statesman and a Utopian reformer, all in one. This diversity of powers did not always find complete equilibrium in his personal life. His activities, therefore, compared to those of Colet and Erasmus, present many more problems and inner tensions. He strove constantly for a way of life suited to his powers, and he wavered between the contemplative quiet of the scholar and a stirring and busy existence, between retirement to a monastery and active participation in English politics. Owing to this variety of interests, More's thought does not present an unbroken line of development. Much that he emphatically maintains in theory, he had to belie as an English political leader. He was himself aware of this inconsistency as he himself has shown clearly enough in his *Utopia.* In this work More distinguishes between a purely abstract philosophy and the *philosophia civilior* which knows its scene of action and how to adapt itself to it, and how to play the role as is becoming and proper in the drama that is momentarily being enacted.

What is required for the third choice of life is a sense of irony, a sense of the difference and yet the relation between the realms of the actual and of the ideal, a consciousness of where one really stands as opposed to where one must appear to stand. Swift, who pretended to have introduced irony, refined it, and showed its use, obviously learned something about it from Thomas More.

Chronology of Important Dates

1667   Swift born in Dublin, of English parents, Nov. 30

1686   B. A., *speciali gratia,* Trinity College, Dublin

1689   Entered, as secretary, service of Sir William Temple at Moor Park; made acquaintance of Esther Johnson (Stella)

1694   Ordained, in Ireland

1695   Presented to the prebend of Kilroot, Ireland

1696   Returned to Moor Park. Temple died in 1699, and Swift began to edit his works

1699   Entered service, as chaplain, of Lord Berkeley, in Dublin. Swift soon began a career as defender of the rights of the Church of Ireland

1704   Published *A Tale of a Tub* and accompanying satires (although, presumably, they were written *ca.* 1697-98)

1710-14   In London, with a brief interval in Ireland, 1713, to be installed as Dean of St. Patrick's Cathedral. Swift edited *The Examiner* and wrote pamphlets in defense of the Tory ministry. *Journal to Stella*

1714   After death of Anne, returned in virtual exile to Ireland, upon the accession of the Whigs

1724   *The Drapier's Letters* published anonymously, in defense of Irish freedom

1726   Visited England; published (anonymously) *Gulliver's Travels*

1728   Death of Stella

1729   Published *A Modest Proposal*

1731   Wrote *Verses on the Death of Dr. Swift*

1745   Died, Oct. 19. Left bequest to found an asylum for the insane

Notes on the Editor and Authors

ERNEST TUVESON, editor of this volume, is a professor of English in the University of California, Berkeley, and author of *Millennium and Utopia: A Study in the Background of the Idea of Progress* (1949), and *The Imagination as a Means of Grace: Locke and the Aesthetics of Romanticism* (1960).

NORMAN O. BROWN's book *Life against Death*, recently reprinted in paperback form, has attracted increasing interest because of its original and perceptive application of psychoanalytic ideas to the interpretation of history.

IRVIN EHRENPREIS, professor of English in the University of Indiana, is currently at work on the most comprehensive biography of Swift yet undertaken.

JOSEPH HORRELL edited the *Collected Poems of Jonathan Swift* for the Muses' Library and has contributed to the *Cambridge Journal* and other scholarly periodicals.

F. R. LEAVIS, whose recent debate with C. P. Snow has attracted wide attention, recently retired as University Reader in English in Cambridge University. His many books of criticism include *Determinations* (1934), *The Great Tradition* (1948), and *The Common Pursuit* (1952).

MAYNARD MACK, the General Editor of the Twentieth Century Views Series, is the author of many studies of eighteenth century literature and of Shakespeare, including the monumental Twickenham Edition of Pope's *An Essay on Man* (1950).

RICARDO QUINTANA, professor of English in the University of Wisconsin, is one of the principal interpreters of Swift.

JOHN F. ROSS is professor of English in the University of California, Los Angeles.

JOHN TRAUGOTT, associate professor of English in the University of California, Berkeley, is the author of *Tristram Shandy's World: Sterne's Philosophical Rhetoric* (1954).

KATHLEEN WILLIAMS, who is on the staff of the University of Leeds, is the author of many articles on Swift, and of *Jonathan Swift and the Age of Compromise* (1958).

Selected Bibliography

THE TEXT

The definitive editions are as follows: *The Prose Works of Jonathan Swift*, edited by Herbert Davis (Oxford; still in progress); *The Correspondence of Jonathan Swift, D. D.*, edited by F. E. Ball (London, 1910-14); and *The Poems of Jonathan Swift*, edited by Harold Williams (Oxford, 1958). In addition, there is the *Journal to Stella*, edited by Harold Williams (Oxford, 1948). A good working collection, with good modern notes and commentary, is that of Louis Landa in paperback, *Gulliver's Travels and Other Writings* (Riverside Editions, 1960).

BIOGRAPHY AND CRITICISM

Case, Arthur E. *Four Essays on "Gulliver's Travels."* Princeton: 1945.

Colie, Rosalie. "Gulliver, the Locke-Stillingfleet Controversy and the Nature of Man." *History of Ideas Newsletter,* II (1956), 58-62. An article that shows how a knowledge of Swift's intellectual environment can illuminate his satire.

Crane, R. S. "The Houyhnhnms, the Yahoos, and the History of Ideas." In *Reason and the Imagination,* edited by J. A. Mazzeo. New York and London: 1962. An attack on many recent interpretations of *Gulliver's Travels.*

Davis, Herbert. *The Satire of Jonathan Swift.* New York: 1947.

Ehrenpreis, Irvin. *The Personality of Jonathan Swift.* London: 1958. A collection of essays refuting several of the common myths about Swift the man.

———. *Swift: The Man, His Works, and the Age.* Vol. I. London: 1962.

Ewald, William B. *The Masks of Jonathan Swift.* Cambridge, Mass.: 1954. The principal study to date of Swift's use of personae.

Firth, Sir Charles. "The Political Significance of 'Gulliver's Travels.'" In *Proceedings of the British Academy,* IX (1920).

Frye, Roland. "Swift's Yahoo and Christian Symbols for Sin." *Journal of the History of Ideas,* XV (1954), 201-17.

Harth, Phillip. *Swift and Anglican Rationalism: The Religious Background of "A Tale of a Tub."* Chicago: 1961.

Kelling, Harold. "*Gulliver's Travels:* A Comedy of Humours." *University of Toronto Quarterly,* XXI (1952), 362-75.

McKenzie, Gordon. "Swift: Reason and Some of its Consequences." In *Five Studies in Literature*, University of California Studies in English, 1940.

Monk, Samuel H. "The Pride of Lemuel Gulliver." *Sewanee Review*, LXIII (1955), 48-71. An important discussion of the moral significance of Swift's greatest satire.

Moore, John B. "The Rôle of Gulliver." *Modern Philology*, XXV (1928), 469-80.

Murry, John Middleton. *Jonathan Swift*. London: 1954.

————. "Swift," in Bibliographical Series of Supplements to *British Book News* on Writers and their Work, 1955.

Nicolson, Marjorie, and Nora Mohler. "The Scientific Background of Swift's *Voyage to Laputa*." Reprinted in Nicolson, *Science and Imagination*, Great Seal Book, 1956. A fascinating study of the materials out of which Swift constructed his satire of the new philosophy.

Price, Martin. *Swift's Rhetorical Art: A Study in Structure and Meaning*. New Haven: 1953.

Quintana, Ricardo. *The Mind and Art of Jonathan Swift*. New York: 1936 (reprinted 1953).

————. *Swift: An Introduction*. London and New York: 1955. This book, and the one cited immediately above, constitute probably the best general survey and analysis of Swift the author and his works.

Starkman, Miriam K. *Swift's Satire on Learning in "A Tale of a Tub."* Princeton: 1950.

Stone, Edward. "Swift and the Horses: Misanthropy or Comedy?" *Modern Language Quarterly*, X (1949), 367-76. Points out that Swift's contemporaries, Pope, and Swift himself, saw the Houyhnhnms and the Yahoos as comic.

Van Doren, Carl. *Swift*. New York: 1930. Still an important critical study, although later research would modify many of its views.

Williams, Kathleen. *Jonathan Swift and the Age of Compromise*. Although rather misleadingly titled, this book is a major study of Swift's understanding and use of the concept of "reason."

TWENTIETH CENTURY VIEWS

British Authors

TWENTIETH CENTURY VIEWS

European Authors

TWENTIETH CENTURY VIEWS

American Authors